The Playgroup Movement

Foreword to the Third Edition

We talk about the playgroup *movement* because learning by active involvement and doing is characteristic at every stage. Involve, in the dictionary, can mean to wind spirally: our learning began with children, spiralled to parents, and then on again to their differing communities.

Rapid growth began to leave PPA supporters unsupported; so a structure was designed that was marvellously like a climbing frame, encouraging people to stretch themselves according to their experience and interests. The appointment of regional Training and Development Officers and more National Advisers led to a new phase of learning as we all worked together, united in our belief that the movement must be eased forward by the continual thrust of the spiral from the playgroups to the national committees.

Now we are back to children, and taking another look at that once joyous and spontaneous word 'play'. There is an old country saying: ' 'urry 'em forrard an' you'll backen 'em'. Surely this is as true for children and their parents as it is for plants and animals. We now see clearly that the more we know what we think about children, play, and childhood as a state in its own right, the better we shall understand how to prepare fieldworkers and tutors. To each new wave of children and parents the playgroup experience is overwhelmingly new and they must not be hurried as they unfold through their learning. We must beware of creating a new 'expertise' lest the depressing turn of the screw from above kills the slow spiral winding growth of both children and parents.

I have faith in the spirit of renewal that still motivates this movement.

Brenda Crowe, November 1976

The Playgroup Movement

by Brenda Crowe
National Adviser, Pre-school Playgroups Association

Published in conjunction with the Pre-school Playgroups Association

London · George Allen & Unwin Ltd
Ruskin House   Museum Street

First published by George Allen & Unwin Ltd 1973
Second edition 1975
Third edition 1977
Original edition published by the Pre-school Playgroups
Association in March 1971

ISBN 0 04 372024 2 hardback
     0 04 372025 0 paperback

Printed in Great Britain
in 11 *point Times Roman type*
by Unwin Brothers Limited
Old Woking, Surrey

Preface

From Lord Belstead, Joint Parliamentary Under Secretary of State, Department of Education and Science

Since 1966, the Department of Education and Science has made a grant to the Pre-school Playgroups Association to enable it to appoint and employ a National Adviser; this Report is one of the results of that appointment. It is full of information and practical advice about the setting up and running of playgroups and the training of playgroup staff and I found it most interesting. It deserves to be widely read.

From W. D. Wall, BA, PhD, Dean of the Institute of Education, University of London; President, Pre-school Playgroups Association

In her years as National Adviser to the Pre-school Playgroups Association, Brenda Crowe has observed playgroups in many different areas. Her work has taken her all over Britain and she has talked not only with playgroup leaders, but with local authority officers and many professional teachers, health visitors, and social workers. Above all, she has talked with mothers and she is writing here about all she has learned.

Playgroups need to be relevant to the communities they serve and it is clear from this report that where they are successful, and involving parents, they are meeting the needs of mothers and children, together.

If we accept that the quality of parental care is the most important factor in a child's development, certainly in his earliest years, then one of our chief concerns should be to support and encourage mothers in their demanding, vital role.

Mrs Crowe makes the case that playgroups provide a most important means of offering this support. We should therefore be looking to see how we can foster their growth so that more

children and parents can benefit, and how we can make professional advice available to them.

In the chapters which deal with playgroup courses, describing
how mothers are learning with great enthusiasm about their
own and other people's children, Mrs Crowe's report points to
ways in which playgroups can become, not a substitute for
other forms of pre-school care, but an essential part of varied
provision for under-fives.

From the report one sees how community-based, parent
co-operative groups could, if they develop along the right lines,
begin to raise standards of mothering. It is an important book
for all in the field, and should do much to stimulate thought
and discussion.

Contents

CONTENTS

CONTENTS

Introduction

The benefits to the children of all good playgroups are these:

Play opportunities are offered that few would have at home, partly because money is lacking for a full range of activities and equipment, but chiefly because parents are unaware of the types of play experience that children need.

Children can learn to communicate with each other, and with adults; and within this framework of warm friendliness speech is stimulated and the use of language can be developed.

The separation from mother can come about slowly and naturally, so that the eventual transition from home to a full day at school will not be accompanied by the physical and emotional exhaustion that many parents have noted in children denied this interim period of preparation.

The transition from a small family unit to a rather larger unit helps the children to grow accustomed to a greater level of noise and movement; it also enables them to learn to co-operate with other children and other adults.

The doses of exposure to all these new experiences can be graded to suit each individual child; two weekly periods of two hours each may be enough for some children at first, and the transition to four or five sessions a week can be as gradual as the child's reaction dictates—providing the extra sessions are available and the housekeeping money stretches this far. The playgroup can be so flexible that many of the children's differing needs can be met individually.

But there is one type of playgroup that stands out by virtue of the many benefits it confers upon all those who come within its orbit. The good community playgroup, firmly rooted in its own locality, offers all the above benefits to the children but also provides stimulation, happiness, and an avenue of growth for the following people.

Mothers (who also happen to be people)

There is a very real need for mothers to go off-duty for a couple of hours occasionally. Who else is on the job for twenty-four consecutive hours, seven days a week, without even a break for meals? There may well be younger children at home, but one child less for two hours twice or three times a week is still a welcome relief, leading to happier reunions.

When their turn for rota duty at the playgroup comes round they find that being with children may be a real joy; they can relax with nothing else to claim their attention, and many begin to 'see' children for the first time. They can watch other adults handle their own and·other people's children, and often learn new insights into old problems. They begin to understand the wide range of growth, temperament and ability in children of three to four years—all of which fall well within the normal limit. They can make friends with other adults in this happy proximity that breaks down what seems to be universal shyness. Those who left school and work with a feeling of failure have the opportunity to discover that they can start learning and growing all over again.

'Just mothers' become rota mothers; rota mothers can become helpers; helpers can become playgroup leaders. The way ahead is free for them to sit on committees, be in charge of milk money or fund-raising, go on to become area organizers or to contribute on courses. Many go on to train as teachers, NNEBs or social workers, even though it sometimes means tackling GCE O and A levels first. Others deliberately go into jobs where the mother/child relationship comes under stress. Such a person feels deeply involved in a children's shoe department, and rejoices when parents and children deliberately seek her out time after time.

Those who feel frustrated in the maternal role can accept it more easily if they have an outlet for their other abilities, and contact with a wide range of people.

There is already evidence that parents are not only learning about the under-fives, but are enjoying a continuing and extending parental role.

14

Fathers (who also happen to be people)

Their financial commitment is heavy, and stretches ahead into the far distant future. On their own they may feel they could have 'made it' by changing jobs, starting up on their own, going abroad. But family responsibilities weigh heavily, and rather than jeopardise present security many men curb their ambitions. Hope is deferred, and can fade.

Not all men take to fatherhood like ducks to water. If their wives aggravate this by giving them the impression that only women know how to handle, feed, and look after babies then the man suffers a double loss as the husband-wife relationship loses out to a baby who does not offer a compensating pleasure.

Many a man who rejoices in fatherhood can still find it disappointing to come home to a wife who is depressed, over-tired or bad tempered. His own day may well have been difficult, and he finds it hard to see what can have been so dreadful about spending all day in the home that he only has a chance to enjoy at weekends.

The father and the mother may disagree about the upbringing of their child; the father may be too firm as he tries to correct what he believes to be his wife's over-indulgence, and he can then find himself with both his wife and child against him. Since mother and child are together all day he can begin to feel an outsider.

The wife may continue to keep up the highest standards for their home, the children and her own personal appearance— but a sensitive husband may be aware that the strain is great. Mechanical or human help, or a holiday, may be out of the question financially and he feels helpless too.

Anything that improves the mother's health and happiness has a profound effect upon her husband and children. The child gains twice over: he grows physically, emotionally, socially and intellectually through his playgroup experience, and comes home to continue growing in a happier, fuller home life than before. This wave of improvement flows yet again, for as the parents see their child developing in so many ways their pleasure and interest grow both in him and in their shared experience as parents, and they feel that they are making out creditably.

Fathers sit on playgroup committees, work together to

improve playgroup buildings and equipment, carry heavy equipment out of sheds and into the playgroup before going to work, organize fund-raising events, and offer encouragement and support to their wives. Many areas have a flourishing social life that brings the playgroup husbands and wives together, both with and without their children. The sharing of baby-sitting is often highly organized on a voucher system.

Men need this mixed company; all too often they have broken with 'the boys' who were so much part of their bachelor existence, and their lives are narrowed down to home and work. This new social life can be rewarding.

Teenagers

The interaction between teenagers and playgroups works its own magic of healing and growth.

These young adolescents need to play in their own right, and in some areas workshops have been set up to give them a chance to make good some of their missing stages of growing-up. This personal play is the springboard for their curiosity and interest when they later find themselves in a playgroup. Play becomes the common bond across the mini-generation gap, for many older children are so sick of looking after younger brothers and sisters that it is some time before they are prepared to say of the children, 'It's funny, but I really like being with them here.'

Young people are also learning by absorption that it is possible for neighbourhood parents to enjoy their children, and to have time to play and talk with them.

Many, particularly from various institutions, long for a way to express tenderness in a relationship where it can't rebound and hurt: in a playgroup affection can both be given and received between children and adults of all ages.

Backward readers can justify the reading of 'baby books' and the listening children's wrapt attention is balm to wounded pride. Nothing succeeds like success, especially after years of failure.

The natural conversation which often flows between the younger and older children can be a salutary reminder to listening adults that interest, relationship and communication can be deadened by artificial conversations directed to the end of Acquisition and Development of Language.

16

We must now be very, very careful not to crush all this happiness, human growth and development under the weight of written work, projects and all the paraphernalia devised to bring about the sort of learning that is already happening through practical experience and discussions in happy neighbourhood relationships.

Mothers and toddlers

By three it is already too late to help some children and their parents, and many playgroups run special sessions for under-threes *and* their accompanying mother. This is not only for the children's sake, but because many mothers feel that they are 'failures' at this point: they long to dump-and-run rather than to stay and risk being shown up by their anti-social offspring. It is only by staying that they are able to discover how universal their problems are, and to experience how the group gathers round newcomers with warm support and good humour, and to see how other people cope with energetic, tyrannical, apathetic, clumsy, mercurial, tempestuous, exhausting and enchanting toddlers.

The over-sixties

Many grandfathers and grannies are happily involved in playgroups, mending toys, knitting or just being grandparent substitutes for families away from their roots. Their satisfaction can be summed up by one who said, 'It's lovely to feel useful and needed again.'

Who matters most?

We cannot say under-fives matter more than any other age group, but as it is now known that fifty per cent of the total intelligence is developed by the age of four years it could be said that they need more attention in these early years. But how can a child be stretched intellectually if he is already an emotional cripple? How can a child be emotionally healthy if there is pressure or apathy in the home? How, in short, can under-fives really be helped to realize their full long-term potential unless the parents are also helped? The needs of children, mothers and fathers are closely interrelated, and the nature of

17

these needs varies not only from one individual to another but from one community to another.

In one area the stimulus and achievement of endless fund-raising is necessary: in another area fund-raising may be less important than creative outlets for those with a growing capacity to shoulder responsibility. In some areas skilled help is needed to draw some mother back into the community; in other areas good-hearted neighbourliness is enough to get the playgroup on its feet.

Anyone wanting to meet the needs of the children must also meet the varying needs of the parents.

What about the standard of play?

The rigid yardstick marked Standard needs, in this situation, to give way to a sliding-scale marked Value. But the one does not preclude the other.

On entering a playgroup the question one asks oneself should be, 'Is this playgroup of positive value to both the children and adults in it, and to the community in which it is set?'

If the playgroup is an area where the children's family and play experience has already been full and rewarding, then the level of play, communication and challenge would need to be very high indeed to offer anything of positive value.

If the playgroup has been started by parents in an area where most families talk very little, where books are unknown, where stimulation is lacking, and where the play needs of children are not understood, then it will take time for the standard of play to rise. In visiting such a playgroup it is essential to take into consideration the value of corporate enthusiasm, the action and involvement, the acceptance of responsibility, and the growth and learning of the parents. The children and parents grow together, and slowly both generations make good missed experiences, and the playgroup learning flows back into the home. Not only are the children offered playgroup activities at home, the mother/child relationship improves and the family becomes more harmonious and positive. The improvement in the mother's health is often dramatic, and this benefits everyone.

The standard will need to improve or the value will decrease as the children grow bored or out of hand, and the adults' confidence and happiness falters. But local advisers need to see to it that their courses are not aimed at such a perfectionist level that the mothers grow anxious and strained. The happiness of all concerned is essential and the standard of play can only rise as quickly as the mothers can put into practice what they learn.

This must not be taken to mean that the quality of play does not matter. It matters very much both for the children's sake and for the mothers whose insight into children will come about through watching them as they play, and in learning what to provide in order to meet the children's needs.

Part I

Understanding Playgroups

Chapter 1

Playgroups for different local needs

The comment heard most frequently from those working in the Departments of Health, Social Services and Education is, 'I'm all in favour of what playgroups are doing, but the tragedy of it is that they're in the areas that don't really need them. It is the deprived areas that concern us.'

Whilst understanding this viewpoint, it is noticeable that it is tending to make many mothers feel guilty about having playgroups in 'nice' areas. This is a pity, for all children and all parents can benefit from a good playgroup.

New insight into the definition of deprivation began to dawn on me after several visits to areas of back-to-back housing, tower flats, and depressing acres of old-type identical council houses. On each occasion the mothers happily involved in playgroups of varying standard all said that they felt guilty at having their playgroup 'because it isn't us middle-class mothers that need it, it's the deprived areas'.

What is middle-class? What is a deprived area?

Not everyone living in a deprived area is a deprived personality; often those designated deprived do not feel themselves to be so—and those regarded as privileged can be aware of deep personal deprivation.

A good playgroup adapts to the needs of its environment, and the major variations between good playgroups seem to provide a clue to the particular local type of deprivation. After a year of checking up on this, it still seems valid. There are obvious weaknesses in trying to classify people into groups—we all know that it cannot be done; nature, nurture, environment, all play their part, and it is the individuality of each person that matters. But in spite of these misgivings, it still seems worthwhile to offer the results of my observations.

AREAS OF MULTIPLE DEPRIVATION

These are the families or lone mothers who live without hope. The men are often in prison or out of work; the women usually give up the battle to fight for standards when so many things militate against them—no housing worthy of the name home; over-crowding or, in rural areas, isolation; no money, or money without the knowledge of how to handle it; an unhappy marriage or liaison; poor health, mentally, physically or both; often too many pregnancies too quickly, because of religious conviction or because their husbands will not let them use contraceptives, or because they are frightened to take the pill, or because they have a supply but forget to take them. Almost all of them truly love their children, but few can cope with them adequately. These mothers have reached the stage of aiming no higher than to get through another day; and some are unable to bring themselves to get out of bed even to try to face another day.

The children in these families are usually fed and clothed inadequately and the habit of grizzling owes much to this background of physical discomfort; almost without exception they love their parents, especially their mothers, and they accept the shouts, slaps and hugs as they come, knowing that they are loved even though they are unable to recognize any pattern in the unpredictable behaviour to which they are subjected. There is little or no conversation, and children may arrive at school unable to talk. Nor is there any stimulation of mind or body.

There seem to be two main ways of helping to establish playgroups in these areas.

1. For the local authorities to start a playgroup for the children. Health visitors and social workers can identify the families, and visits to the homes pave the way for transport to call to collect the children and take them to the playgroup that has been set up to receive them. In local authority playgroups the equipment is provided, the rent is paid, and a salary is paid to the permanent playgroup leader and her assistant.

Even given transport, however, some mothers cannot make

the effort to get up and take the child out to the waiting car or van. The drivers expect this, open the door and call—and sometimes even dress the child. If the mothers have reached this level of despair, it can take one, or even two, years before they dare to believe that something nice is happening at last; they begin, cautiously, to look forward to seeing the van drive up, and are waiting to have a word or two when it returns. Some of these mothers eventually go into the playgroup, meet other mothers and begin to pick up. But many remain unable to respond.

Playgroups of this type are being run in both urban and rural areas by the Save the Children Fund, local authorities, the Pre-school Playgroups Association, the National Society for the Prevention of Cruelty to Children, the National Elfrida Rathbone Association and other local groups of people.

2. To start Mothers' Clubs. The mothers find it much easier to respond in this situation, where they feel that someone is caring about *them*, with no strings attached. Since they cannot leave their pre-school children at home, plans have to include a playgroup.

So, in effect, two playgroups are born simultaneously: one for mothers, another for children.

Nothing less than sound common sense, allied to genuine caring, will draw the mothers together and hold them. Social workers are invaluable here, and a few other men and women who have the ability to accept these mothers as they are and who are prepared to create a happy environment with no hint of sentimentality or do-gooding, or making-them-more-adequate.

Where these groups are in existence the improvement in morale is quite dramatic. Tea and chat are enough for some weeks, and then things begin to happen. Surprisingly, some of these mothers begin to say, 'Now I'm here, I might as well go and see the dentist (or doctor).' Talks are requested; one group asked the butcher back again because he was so helpful over which bits of the animal came from where, and how to cook them; another popular visitor was a woman who taught them all to knit, which they found both soothing and satisfying. (She also showed them how to cut the sleeves off a jumper, sew

25

up the neck, turn the garment upside down, run elastic round the top, and hey-presto!—new trousers!)

And what about the children? Sometimes local volunteers, with no knowledge of playgroups, have offered to look after the children while the social workers and others are with the mothers. A few books, some dolls and plasticine are on offer, and all goes well for a while; the children are usually apathetic at first, and some are more than content just to be cuddled; but then the boys begin to get the situation taped, and feel secure enough to start rushing around making gun and tractor noises— and nobody feels secure any more. The noise is exhausting and the helpers hang on with one eye on the clock, taking comfort from the fact that 'they must need it badly, or they wouldn't keep it up like this, would they?'

This sort of playgroup is inadequate. The mothers, having had a lovely afternoon, collect their children to go home—and their new-found peace of mind is shattered by hysterically wound-up children who do not respond until the old, familiar 'Shut-up!' or 'Come here!' are shouted at them as before. Back to square one. And it's a case of hanging on as before until the next week's high spot. The mother's enjoyment has been abruptly terminated. Some of the children may have found a certain amount of satisfaction to the detriment of others, but no real play has been provided for their needs at all.

This situation may be avoided where a well-equipped and adequately staffed playgroup is prepared for the children. Numbers must be watched, for twenty mothers can bring over fifty under-fives; with fewer than twenty mothers it may feel flat instead of feeling like a party. But this number of children, among whom will be several babies, will need more than one room. Youth centres and community halls can sometimes offer splendid accommodation, with rooms for the babies and toddlers, a room or hall for the playgroup, a canteen for the mothers, and small rooms for those mothers who want to talk to the social workers privately. Then everyone can go home happy and satisfied.

In one such pocket of deprivation the Pre-school Playgroups Association area organizer worked with the social worker and senior nursing officer to prepare a proper playgroup as an integral part of the project. Equipment was begged, borrowed and improvised, and in one youth centre this was stored under the stage even though dolls' clothes and dressing-up clothes had to be kept in plastic bags to protect them from the damp. Expendable items such as paint, paper and dough were provided each time by the playgroup helpers who volunteered to staff the playgroup with PPA's voluntary organizer.

These experienced playgroup people learned a great deal from this new experience. One child painted timidly, and the playgroup leader said, 'How lovely! Shall we go and show it to mummy?' They went to find the mother who glanced at the offering, screwed it up, dropped it on the floor, and continued her chat to her neighbour without, apparently, noticing the child at all. The following week, having learned from this incident, the playgroup leader left the child painting and went to find the mother to tell her that her son was busily painting a picture especially for her. The mother responded to this friendly approach, and they chatted for a few minutes until the playgroup leader said that she would go and see if the work of art was finished: when she re-appeared with the child and his wet and colourful offering the mother looked up and smiled, the child ran to put the painting on her lap (where she let it rest) and after this brief but warm encounter he returned to the other room to paint again.

Mothers need to be helped to play their part in a playgroup and eventually, when the occasional mother pops into the other room to see what is going on, she finds the children happy and busy playing with sand, water, clay, dough, paint, bricks, table toys, climbing frames, etc. For the first time she sees what real play is, and what a difference it makes to children: when they go home together their mutual satisfaction and happiness is shared for a moment. Gradually, some of the mothers gravitate to the playgroup for no other reason than that they suddenly find they enjoy being with the children, and the more they come to understand, the greater chance there is that this harmony will be carried back into the home.

The playgroup people also learned that although children may be aged four-and-a-half years, their stage of play may correspond to the average child of eighteen months; they are neither naughty nor silly if they suck bricks, bang them together or throw them. In the early days jig-saw puzzles and books may well be ignored, and the helpers' normal vocabulary and speed of speaking may be met with blank incomprehension.

The continuous backing of the social worker is essential; the holding needs to go on and so, too, will individual casework. These groups are an aid to casework, even a preventative, but they cannot be a complete substitute for individual home visits.

In time, some of the mothers may want to assume more responsibility in the playgroup—but it must be when *they* are ready. They must come to this out of their own discovery that the children like them and respond to them, and that they enjoy being with children under these circumstances. It must never be assumed that these mothers are not capable of personal growth; but neither should anything be demanded.

AREAS AT A DISADVANTAGE

It is not possible to make sweeping generalizations, but some housing estates fall within this category. The mothers may not be down-and-out, but many of them are certainly down; they are often terribly lonely, unable to cope with the children (and unwilling to stop trying to cope), short of money, or unable to budget. They may feel trapped because no stage in their lives has brought the happiness and fulfilment that they confidently expected would come eventually. So there they are, with a home, a husband, children and nothing else to look forward to, as far as they can see. And there seems an awful lot of life still to be got through.

These are some of the ways in which I have seen this problem tackled.

1. Someone on the spot starts a playgroup, working with a small nucleus of interested mothers. Often it is the wife of the vicar or minister or an experienced playgroup leader, in consultation with the health visitor. The playgroups often start with small numbers, and gradually enlarge as news spreads by word of mouth. By the time the numbers are rising, the original group of mothers has had time to learn from its mistakes, and has often visited nursery schools and other playgroups in order to check what they are doing. They attend informal meetings, and progress to join local playgroup courses, with enthusiasm.

2. Occasionally money can be provided for a regular playgroup leader. It could come from a local charity; or the local authority; or the local branch of PPA. However it is done, the point to bear in mind is the importance of appointing a playgroup leader *who understands how necessary it is to involve the mothers*. Only by being in a well-run playgroup can mothers begin to see what real play can be, and what it can do to a child; only by being there can they see how the playgroup leader copes with shyness, aggression, jealousy, timidity, curiosity, excitement, bossiness, children who take things, children who tell lies. Although many mothers demand that their children say 'Please', 'Pardon' and 'Thank you', it sometimes has not occurred to them to be equally courteous to the children; sometimes they have never seen how helpful and dependable three-year-olds can be; sometimes they do not know how much or how little to expect from the children.

This is why the choice of a playgroup leader is so important. Not only does she need to be able to respond to the needs of children, she needs to be able to do it in such a way that the mothers unthinkingly begin to copy her. She needs to be sensitive to the needs of the mothers; to be a friend and a leaning post; to know how to guide the running of the play-group in such a way that the mothers feel that it is *their* play-group; to know when, and to whom, to delegate responsibility in order that each shall grow in stature and discover that she is capable of far more than she thought.

Again and again, before the playgroup came into being, the health visitors, social workers, Pre-school Playgroups Associa-tion area organizers and others tell me that the constant cry of the mothers was 'But I can't do anything like that!' and their response was 'But of course you can! Have a go!' And they did; and they can.

3. Sometimes a group of mothers will come together, after much morale boosting by the health visitors, vicar, minister, priest, social worker, or other playgroup enthusiast, and decide to have a bash at it themselves. They know that 5p a morning is all they can budget for, and realizing that this will not pay even a token payment to a playgroup leader, they decide to work in pairs to run the group, with other mothers to make up the extras to meet the staffing ratio.

Such playgroups caused me grave concern: where was the security? The weaknesses are obvious: the children never know who is going to be in charge; different adults have different standards; emotions may well run high between the adults as they argue about the merits of a good smack against banishment to the kitchen as a punishment; conflict is likely to arise over the care of precious equipment; free play is likely to be interpreted as playing about; lack of both money and knowledge may well lead to tatty and inadequate equipment; no child's progress, or distress, can be followed up; the group could grow increasingly wild as each pair of mothers thinks, 'Thank goodness it's only two or three times a term!'

My overall concern remains. But some areas are turning a potentially disastrous situation into a venture that is proving valuable for both the children and the mothers. In this sort of situation, wise background help is needed from the beginning and the visitor needs to understand clearly that the personal growth in understanding and responsibility of the mothers is of the utmost importance. *Everything else will stem from this.* This means that one of the attributes most needed by visitors (whether professionally employed or voluntary) is their rapport with such mothers—a knowledge of play and under-fives alone is not enough.

In other areas local authorities have appointed social development officers. One of the earliest is now the proud father of many well-established playgroups. This man's particular gift lies in his ability to lead from the rear: it takes imagination to foresee the next likely crisis and to prepare for it behind the scenes.

A playgroup started by a group of mothers without preparation could well be a free-for-all. But in one area a plan slowly unfolded that started with coffee evenings to plan fund-raising events; the events were fun, as well as hard work; the spending of the money was important, so 'What about a nursery school teacher to come and discuss things with us?' So far so good. The mothers were invited to go and spend time in the nursery school, which they loved, but the sight of the equipment filled everybody with envy. A gloomy coffee evening led to yet another fund-raising event, and also to a suggestion that everybody should start to make, mend and improvise equipment. An evening making dolls' clothes and dressing-up clothes can, with the right tutor, start people thinking along the lines of real play and also child development—some clothes need large buttons for little fingers, others can have large hooks and eyes.

So, slowly, the original course developed almost without people being aware of the fact. In this area courses are now accepted as a necessary preliminary for the mothers of all the children about to form a playgroup. These courses are free, and are held as far as possible at or near the place where the playgroup will meet; the tutors try to follow the group through supportive visits during the first few weeks of its existence, and this is done voluntarily because they care.

It bears repeating that the essential need in this sort of situation is for a mature, ever available, background figure who knows when to delegate and withdraw; and the constant need is to balance the needs of both the children and the mothers. *In our right concern to provide the best possible environment for the under-fives we must be careful not to make their mothers feel unworthy and inadequate.* Common kindness suggests that it is unreasonable to devote all our giving to the children. Many mothers have not received enough themselves, and how can you give if you have not first received?

Whoever starts these playgroups must constantly arrange to be present at the extra occasions which are planned to give something positive to the mothers and, indirectly, to the children. It may be a visit to a good playgroup a mini-bus drive away, in preference to one considerably nearer; it will cost more money, but the dividend is likely to be high. The anticipation of a day out gives a kick to the preceding week; the feeling of being dressed-up and out on a spree is lovely; there is always something to be learned from visiting a new playgroup and the long journey home offers the opportunity to discuss what has been seen and to decide what alterations could be made to their own playgroup.

Children in these groups do not, at first, have the standard of play that they would have in a 'good' playgroup—but in drawing up a profit and loss account it has to be remembered that the mothers' handling of their children at home has taken a stride forward; and that the new interest has provided a real growing-point for both parents, for the improvement in a wife's morale benefits the husband and other children—and many husbands respond by taking an interest in this new venture that is paying such dividends in all-round happiness.

Another item in the profit column is the clamour for more and more playgroup courses—and this is proving to be as rewarding and stimulating for the tutors as it is for mothers. All the tutors say, 'These mothers are marvellous; they are so eager to learn and are so responsive.' The evidence seems clear: the mothers want to learn and they can and do learn; the standard of play can and does rise. And the relationships between the mothers and their children often improve dramatically. But other problems do have to be considered.

FIRST GENERATION HOME OWNERS

Generalization is particularly inaccurate here, for the range is wide. However, for many couples it is the first time that anyone in their family has been in a financial position to plan a regular payment for twenty years ahead. Advertising pressure is too strong for many of them—they long to have all the right new things to go in their new homes, and hire purchase commitments add to the already heavy monthly repayment of the mortgage. The pride and strain of ownership are so great that it is surely understandable (though unfortunate) when children are forbidden to play either indoors or out: dirtiness becomes naughtiness. The parents tend to feel that everyone else in the road can afford things more easily than they can, and there is real anxiety that they will not be accepted by the community. Their anxiety is paralleled by that of their children—love becomes conditional, 'Mummy and Daddy will love me if I'm good'; and good seems to involve being clean, quiet and clever.

Playgroup leaders in these areas all have the same tale to tell: the parents set great store by education (it was passing the eleven-plus that enabled them to get to grammar school, making possible the good job and the mortgage), and they are anxious that their children shall be prepared for school so fully that, even if there are forty in the admission class, their child will get off to a good start. There is nothing wrong with this desire to use the pre-school years to the best advantage. The tragedy is that 'the best' tends to be 'that which one can see and hear'. Great pressure is put upon playgroup leaders to 'get them on', to 'teach them just the first things about reading and number', to 'make little things, like they do down the road at Mrs X's nursery school'.

How it would help if the title nursery school were reserved only for those establishments run by fully qualified nursery school teachers, and approved by the Department of Education and Science. It is difficult for the playgroup leader to explain, to the parents' satisfaction, why their playgroup does not churn out an end-product for each day's play; the parents think she is making excuses. Many a playgroup leader in this position asks the head of the local infants' school if she would come and talk to the parents. Once a head mistress says, 'No formal work, and "messes" are right at this age', the mothers believe her.

These mothers benefit greatly from helping in a playgroup; often they have come from an extended family, but have moved as part of bettering themselves, with consequent isolation. In the friendly atmosphere of a group their confidence comes back, in fact they can be over-confident, for they are unaware of their lack of understanding about children's play needs. The cry tends to be 'Come here, and I'll show you how to make a rabbit!' The playgroup leader constantly finds herself anticipating and deflecting such moves by oblique guidance such as, 'Would you like to go and sit near the painting? We never say anything to the children, we like them to paint without even knowing that we are there—but when they've finished and gone off, someone needs to be there to put their name on it (in case they want to take it home) hang it up to dry, and pin up a fresh piece of paper for the next child.'

These mothers are particularly rewarding on courses. Once they like and trust the tutor, and discover that much of her experience has also been theirs, then they are prepared to let go many of their misconceptions and to re-learn. The tutor's responsibility is great here, for once the trust is given many will believe anything that she says without question. It would be all too easy to substitute one set of rigid conventions for another.

RACIALLY-MIXED AREAS

It is hoped that children and their parents in these areas will be drawn into the nearest playgroup, without it being called a 'multi-racial playgroup'.

This is not quite the same thing as saying that no more thought has to be given to these playgroups than to any others. Considerable thought needs to be given to several matters.

Language

In many cases the children have no language but their own, and the adults in the group need to come together to discuss just how they can best help. For example, in one playgroup a child who knew no English was settling happily into the group, and had reached the stage of making warm contact with the adults by going up to them to show a painting, a hat from the dressing-up box, a completed puzzle, or some other offering. In every case the adults' response was a beaming smile, and the word 'Lovely!' Their desire to be simple, direct, and welcoming was thoughtful—up to a point. But what a bewildering all-purpose word 'lovely' must have seemed to the child.

House groups are proving to be helpful for children of many nationalities, and some parents choose a small group deliberately until the foundation of a second language is laid down.

Dress

Most of the children wear European dress, but many of the mothers do not. It is thoughtful to include among the dressing-up clothes and dolls' clothes some that will be familiar to everyone wanting to 'be mother' in the home corner.

Books and pictures

Everyone should be able to find pictures of children, adults, animals and countries that speak to their own personal experience.

Music and songs

Each country has its own cultural roots; and where parents keep their heritage alive it is to be hoped that the playgroup will be a place where it can be shared. In some groups immigrant mothers (from several countries) pay visits to the playgroup to sing their traditional songs—and great is the joy of the children who try to learn to sing in a new language.

Social customs

Care is needed here, and first-hand knowledge from someone in the community. The golden rule for children is that no one shall divide their loyalty to their parents. If the child's up-bringing tells him that certain things, or customs, are forbidden, then no pressure should be put upon him to conform to a different standard. In time he may come to accept that certain things are 'right' in some places, for some people. He may even feel free to join in. But the parents' wishes must be both under-stood and respected.

Religion

Playgroup leaders need to understand something of the religious background of the children in their care, particularly the prac-ticalities relating to eating and fasting. This is especially important if parents are to be happily involved both in the playgroup and, socially, outside it.

The need of these immigrant children is very great indeed: many of them will enter school still unable to talk in the language by which they will be taught.

Sometimes individuals or groups start a playgroup that could be of particular help to these children, but are hampered by lack of finance. One example will serve to illustrate the prob-lems. A prosperous market town has pockets of real human need; the situation of one such small area was particularly distressing on account of several language barriers as well as poverty. The local PPA branch decided to start a playgroup and divided the ground-work between them: the mothers were asked if they would like a playgroup, and responded with cautious optimism; a hall was found, even though the daunting minimum rent was £1 per session. Money was raised, £35 from a charitable trust, £10 by donation, £40 by a branch appeal; equipment was donated by local playgroups or bought by individuals, and one playgroup ran a coffee evening and donated a rocking boat bought with the proceeds.

The PPA county organizer and her friend, who also tutored playgroup courses, undertook to be the permanent playgroup leaders, and seven people volunteered as helpers, for at this stage they were unable to involve the local mothers.

The playgroup opened for one morning and one afternoon a week. For the morning session the children attended from 9.30–12; the playgroup leaders and helpers arrived at the hall at 9.15, and left at 12.30 (the total distance travelled by them was fifty-four miles, and the total cost was 78p, plus one car journey). The afternoon session was from 1.30–3.30 for the children, and from 1.15–4 for the playgroup leaders and helpers (plus the same travelling costs, time and money).

The first week saw five children in the playgroup but then, slowly, more began to attend: two Indians, one West Indian, three Yugoslavs, one half-German, and seven English children who were almost as inarticulate as the others. The very high ratio of adults to children was needed; before language can be learned a personal relationship has to be formed. The warmth of the relationships began to draw the mothers near, and at the time of writing it is judged that the moment has come when the mothers are ready to enjoy coming together one evening to discuss a parent rota in the playgroup. It even seems hopeful that some of the mothers may be ready to come together on 'a sort of committee', and that they would enjoy six or so preliminary evenings of experimenting with and discussing the activities offered to their children in the playgroup.

The children pay 5p each session, handed over at the time (nothing is paid in the event of absence). The prospect of continuous fund raising in order to pay the £1 rent per session was too formidable to be feasible. And diligent inquiries (backed by the positive proof that the venture was both possible and valuable) led to the renting of another hall, where the cost was expected to be between 25p and 50p per session. Meanwhile, the branch continues to raise funds; the volunteers continue to pay their own fares and offer their services free; and the mothers themselves are beginning to feel so involved that they want to help with money-raising efforts themselves.

What is the future of the group? It seems unlikely that the mothers will be able to run it themselves unless they can raise the money to pay for a regular playgroup leader—which, clearly, they will not be able to do. So the present arrangement must continue; the volunteers are prepared for this, and have no intention of failing these newly-enthused mothers. But as a long-term arrangement it is unsatisfactory.

On being asked if she thought there was any realistic hope of starting more playgroups in this area, the founding playgroup leader replied, 'Only if you can get someone to take the initiative in starting it. Once started I've found people quite eager to help but I may have been exceptionally lucky. People of my age, provided they like the work of course, have more time than young mothers. I and two others of our group of helpers are in our later fifties.'

Money is urgently needed to provide a permanent playgroup leader for this first group, in order that this particular woman may be freed to go and start a new group.

If some of the Urban Aid money were given to the Pre-school Playgroups Association then projects such as this could be stabilized quickly.

In theory, application can be made for money from Urban Aid for pockets of deprivation, but the time-lag before the request is approved and the money is made available renders it impossible for many individual schemes to benefit.

Some playgroups in the areas of greatest need can start because the right person is in the right place at the right time—and she acts.

But once the project is instigated, launched, and stabilized it needs money to ensure continuity.

In other cases there may be no local PPA branch to back up the project and provide the initial starting grant, and here money could be provided earlier, providing there was reasonable evidence that the project was a solid possibility and not an idealist's pipe dream.

HIGH FLATS

It is more than disturbing to talk with a mother living in a seventh floor flat with three children under five. The mother's problems are loneliness; fear of accidents involving windows, balconies, stairs and lifts; fear of getting too friendly with next-door neighbours 'in case they get so friendly that they're popping in all the time!'; the cut-off feeling that comes from never seeing anything pass your window but the occasional bird or plane; the tendency to stay in the flat, 'It's such a performance to get the pram and baskets and children in and out of the doors and up and down the lifts'; lack of fresh air, 'You don't even go down to the drying ground after a bit, people nick your washing. Anyway, what are you to do if it rains—belt down with the baby, the toddler and the clothes basket?' The number one complaint seems to be 'my nerves'. Incredibly, although the mothers are so strained, some manage to make a near-normal life for their children: 'I shop twice a day so that I can always say, "We'll be going out soon." '

Children who show a marked reaction at the playgroup tend to do it in different ways. They have been so cramped in the flat that all they want to do is to race up and down until they fall, exhausted and blissful, rosy and wet with perspiration. Or they monopolize a bike or scooter, or climb vigorously all over the climbing frame. Playgroup leaders tell me that this often goes on for about two weeks and then they begin to have eyes for other things.

Sometimes the children are so apathetic that they are unable to respond to anything at first. I saw one child with an arm hooked over a rail of the climbing frame, his body half-resting on the bar below—he just leaned there from the time of arrival until milk time, not even watching the others—he seemed completely detached. He did follow the rest to the tables, and watched music and movement with some interest afterwards.

Some children cannot venture into a large room at all. One perceptive and imaginative playgroup leader created a series of flat-sized rooms with rows of chairs; a different activity was put in each, and the children went into the little pens quite happily. I was told that after a while they began to survey the playgroup through the chair legs, and eventually they were able to move out into the big space themselves.

This same playgroup leader always arranged for her rota mothers to be at the door to help with undressing and dressing the children. She felt that this gave the mothers the maximum opportunity to meet each other. One such mother said to me, 'You get to know people by sight, and then when you see them in the supermarket it's easy to smile; and then you can start

38

talking.' As the shyness of the new mother lessens so, without realizing it, she begins to absorb the atmosphere of the play-group; later still she becomes really interested in what the children are doing.

One concerned mother started a playgroup solely for the children of flat-dwellers: she passed the word round to one or two, as she felt it would be wise to start with low numbers. Half an hour after opening the doors there were sixty-three children in the hall. She was deeply distressed at having to turn so many away the following day.

RURAL AREAS

There are several problems in these areas. Isolation, not only of villages from each other, but of individual farmhouses and scattered farm cottages, is one. The children may literally have no one to play with at all, and the situation may be aggravated further if the isolation is distressing to the mother as well. A child and mother living in such close proximity may become over-dependent on each other, or friction may develop in the tension. The emotional health of each is at risk.

Social workers and educational personnel, as well as play-group people, have told me of their concern at the children's inability to speak. One Director of Education said that he was further concerned because in his county the children often entered school able neither to speak nor walk properly. So much of their pre-school life is spent in a pram in the corner of a field while the mother works that their physical and intellectual development are often quite seriously impaired.

In the villages the family is still usually a unit, with grand-mothers often exerting a strong influence on the young mothers. Playgroups are often condemned—'Dad and I brought up seven and we didn't even have water laid on. You've got all the labour-saving gadgets, and only two children, and you should be ashamed if you can't manage them on your own.'

Many deeply rural areas have suddenly found themselves inundated by 'foreigners' as factories move out of the big towns and bring their labour force with them; or a village suddenly becomes a dormitory for a neighbouring town and up go the houses and in flock the bright and enterprising young

39

townsfolk. This causes trouble in many parts of the country. These lively newcomers want to get something started for their own children and for local children—they look forward to being part of the village community. Playgroups do not catch on at first so the new enthusiasts say, 'Well, let's start something for the parents first, a dramatic group; a tennis club; let's raise money for a cricket and football pavilion.' Their motives are genuine, but they fail to see that the speed and vigour with which they propose to tackle problems are anathema to country folk, whose pace is historically geared to that of the herd of cows and the horse-drawn plough. We take tractors for granted, but the present grandfathers certainly spent their days following horses up and down the fields, and the present parents spent their early lives in this slow tempo and rhythm of movement. They think they have broken away from an out-dated past—until the townsfolk arrive; then they know instinctively that they cannot be rushed. So they dig in their heels in bewilderment and anxiety, backed by the certainty that they are right because they belong.

This can, and does, flare into ugliness occasionally, and the villages are split into 'Them' and 'Us'. It is to the credit of the newcomers that they are so often able to retrieve this situation once they understand it. Many of the newcomers in different areas have said, 'We just didn't understand, we were too quick, and too pressing—but we couldn't afford to wait, our children want something now.'

There are three possible ways in which this situation may be tackled.

By working through someone in the village who is respected and trusted. Explain to the health visitor, the head of the local school, the vicar, whoever is interested in the life of the village, what it is that is needed—but begin along the lines, 'Do you think it would be possible to . . . ?' If the idea is launched and supported by one of the trusted inhabitants, all else will follow more smoothly. Remember that the village's way of life is threatened by the newcomers' ideals, just as much as they feel threatened by the inaction of the village people.

If the playgroup starts as a village venture, all the children are more likely to be involved; if it is started by the newcomers only, then it may be a long time before the village children attend.

By establishing a playgroup in a central village, a shuttle service will evolve to collect the children and bring them in. This is happening in many areas. Mothers will sometimes drive fifteen miles to collect children more-or-less on their way to the playgroup. But what of the mothers who have no car, and are not on anyone's route to the playgroup?

By providing playvans to go out to isolated villages and introduce playgroups to them. A van can be stacked with equipment and driven by a peripatetic playgroup leader; she meets a group of mothers and children at their local village hall, they help her to unload, she shows them how to lay out the room and run a play session, and at the end of the morning they help her to reload. The aim is to encourage the parents to take over the running of the playgroup themselves when they are ready, so freeing the van to extend its services and add new villages to its round.

This scheme poses certain problems.

1. The advantage of being presented with the services of an experienced playgroup leader and the equipment could be off-set by the disadvantage of taking this help for granted. It is important that early discussions with all those about to be involved are based firmly on the understanding that the play-group is immediately responsible for the rent and heat of the hall, and also a token payment towards the playgroup leader's salary (equal in amount to what they will eventually pay their own playgroup leader).

It is also important that everyone understands that this regular financial commitment must continue even if half the children are away with measles. Unless this is understood kindness may prevail over realism, and the mothers may feel that it would not be fair to charge anyone who was away.

2. Committee may be a word, not an experience, to most of the parents and it may be wiser to encourage everyone to work together informally in the early stages of the venture.

3. Isolated communities can have their own strong character-istics, and the structure that suits one village may not be

welcome in another. This means that the experience of setting up the first playgroup may not avail the playgroup leader in a different situation. The first year will be particularly taxing to her ingenuity.

4. The idea of a playgroup may well be incomprehensible to the older generation, and requests for such things as storage facilities for big equipment in the village hall could meet with refusal if they are made too soon. In practical terms this will mean that funds raised to start building up equipment for the village's own playgroup will have to be banked, or used to purchase small equipment that can be stored in such cupboard space as may be provided. Confidence and understanding must be built up slowly and responsibly.

It takes time and patience to establish a first-class playgroup. All those about to be involved need preparatory practical sessions; they will need time to absorb how the playgroup leader copes with activities, children and mothers; they will need practice in preparing the room and managing each activity in turn; they will need help and guidance as they undertake the management of the rota of helpers, the liaison with the local school and church, the hall committee and its caretaker and other users. They will need another playgroup course after they have had time to discover from their personal experience that managing the individual activities is only the beginning of learning how to run a good playgroup.

It takes time to establish the routine that children help to clear away, that they sweep up the sand and mop up spills, that chairs are carried with the legs pointing downwards, that sand is not thrown, that dressing-up clothes are hung on pegs. The playgroup leader will have to stay with each group until these standards become habit, and the mothers are confident and able to maintain these standards.

If four playgroups were firmly established during the first year, it would be a triumph for all concerned. Even when they are established they will still need visits to encourage and boost morale from time to time. The nearest PPA branch can help in this, especially if the branch meetings are occasionally held in these villages, or transport from them organized for meetings elsewhere.

SMALL COLONIES OF ACADEMICS

In areas round universities, research stations, etc. there are small concentrations of university staff and specialists. The children of these families tend to be fluent, with a good vocabulary at an early age. This can sometimes be misleading, and it is all too easy to assume that their understanding matches their vocabulary; it is even easier to assume that their emotional age is also at this level. For example, if a four year old can converse easily and intelligently about sparking plugs, thermometers and magnets, it can seem incongruous for him suddenly to fly into a rage because he has been given the wrong mug at milk time. It can call forth the spontaneous comment from a parent, 'Don't be childish!' I have heard playgroup leaders say of some of these children, 'They are marvellous to talk to, you feel you are talking to an equal—but then they'll be completely babyish and roll about on the floor talking baby-talk.'

It seems as though these children can be grown up for just so long, and then they need to regress for a while to recover. It could be tempting to try to feed their apparently insatiable desire for knowledge, to 'stretch' them, as they seem to be intelligent—and the child may try to keep up in order to please. It would also be easy to be slightly shocked at emotional outbursts that seemed so unreasonable. The leaders in these playgroups need to be warmly accepting and to allow those children who need it (and certainly not all do) to regress from talking about water levels, siphoning, etc. to simple, soothing tipping, filling and dabbling.

Some of the mothers find that bringing up children is unexpectedly difficult because they have absorbed so much theory which is unrelated to practice. One young mother said, 'What's the matter with us? We have children who give every evidence that they're going to be highly intelligent at two-and-a-half years and then they wet their beds at twelve.' Other mothers often show real insight as they compare notes with each other, and watch the children in the playgroup.

In such communities there is a need to broaden the social range of playgroups in order that parents and children alike may learn the value of others as people and avoid judgments made on the basis of intellectual qualities alone.

Chapter 2

Playgroups for different family needs

HANDICAPPED CHILDREN

From the handicapped child's point of view the greatest benefit comes from being included in a normal playgroup, for it is the all-pervading normality that works its own brand of healing. But those with no personal experience of having a handicapped child should be a little wary of prescribing too glibly for people who are emotionally involved in this issue. It is clearly apparent that some mothers find it impossible to face a playgroup full of more fortunate mothers and children.

There are a growing number of playgroups started especially for handicapped children, and it is noticeable that the founding member is very often the mother of a handicapped child herself. It is precisely because both she and her husband have been able to rise above their distress that they are able to bring together parents who are in a similar situation. This coming together is a first step into the community, even though it is still a restricted community. In time, and with encouragement, some are able to move out into fuller community life.

Mental and physical handicap

Many playgroups take one, occasionally two, physically or mentally handicapped children. They report that the children improve in almost all cases, and in some the improvement is dramatic. Naturally, where there is improvement the mother's morale is boosted, and this reflects back into the home. Even in those cases that show little or no improvement the mothers seem to find relief in discovering that they and their children are still accepted by the community.

44

PPA's evidence to the National Bureau for Co-operation in Child Care working party on handicapped children showed clearly the value of playgroups to many of these children and their parents. The ordinary playgroup children almost always accept those who are handicapped without apparently thinking that they are different. Noses are wiped solicitously, children are led by the hand to the toilet, the random knocking down of castles is quietly accepted, or the comment will be, 'He didn't mean to do it, did he?'

But two notes of caution need to be sounded.

1. Sometimes the success of one child inspires the local G.P. or health visitor to send several other handicapped children. The ratio of 1:10 shouldn't be exceeded if maximum benefit to every one is to be achieved—and even this ratio will often call for extra helpers. Sometimes the degree of handicap is such that the ratio of 1:20 should not be exceeded.

It must be recognized that some playgroup leaders and playgroup mothers feel unable to include such a child, and no pressure should be put on them to do so. These handicapped children and their mothers are often particularly sensitive to atmosphere and will sense the slightest feeling of revulsion, however carefully it is hidden.

2. Sometimes no medical support or guidance is offered to the playgroup leaders. They usually express their anxiety by saying, 'If only I knew what to expect, and how to help!' Expert guidance would make the responsibility easier to bear. Playgroup leaders need simple directions such as 'Encourage the use of that leg as naturally as possible'; or 'Try unobtrusively to see that he doesn't put too much weight on that leg'; or even such simple advice as 'Don't raise your voice, the blind child often has superior rather than inferior hearing.' Those of us who are professionals in any field tend to forget how much we had to learn ourselves in the early days. We expect far too much of others. They need help at a vary basic level.

Social handicap

Each local authority has its own At Risk Register, and many children on it come into this category: the isolated child, the child of handicapped parents, the child who came late in the family and who is treated like a living doll by much older brothers and sisters, the child from a generally poor environment. It is the latter category where particular care is needed before the child is placed in a playgroup. Whoever refers the child should first visit the playgroup and meet the playgroup leader and rota mothers, for unless they truly welcome the child the plan is unlikely to be satisfactory.

In some areas the mothers have bettered themselves and feel threatened by the presence of a child who revives memories that they are striving to forget. They feel 'it isn't right to include such children in a group like this', and in these circumstances it is wiser, for the child's sake, to seek another playgroup.

One other factor needs to be noted. Some children seem to have an almost animal aversion to the smell of stale urine; to say that the children who object have taken their cue from disapproving adults is, I think, an over-simplification of the case. The experience of several playgroup leaders as well as my own leads me to believe that there is a genuine aversion to the smell in many cases—especially where it is previously unknown. One such child in a group may find himself left out in a way that doesn't happen to physically or mentally handicapped children. And it takes a truly accepting playleader to integrate the mother of such a child. But it *can* be done.

Emotional handicap

The strongest possible warning is needed before any such child is placed in a playgroup, particularly if he falls within the clinical definition of maladjusted.

Many playleaders find that normal aggression is as much as they can cope with (and sometimes rather more), and a child referred to as being beyond his mother's control may be further damaged rather than helped. Such a child, when moving out into the community for the first time, needs to feel secure, to know where the limits are going to be set for him, to know that he will not be allowed to hurt others or himself—and to know that these limits are going to be set with loving firmness, not anger or punishment. If this does not happen, then he gets the reputation of being difficult at the playgroup as well as in the home—and this is a poor start to life in general, and school in particular.

No such child should be placed in a playgroup unless some-one knowledgeable (preferably from the Child Guidance Clinic) has visited the playgroup to ascertain that the group is well established, happy and stable; that the playgroup leader is gifted in handling difficult children, and does not even consider them to be difficult; and that the parents involved are mature enough to accept the child with tolerance and affection, whilst taking the same attitude towards his behaviour as that of the playgroup leader.

CHILDREN IN HOSPITAL

There were pioneers taking play to children in hospitals long before the playgroup movement gathered its present momentum, notably the Save the Children Fund. During the last decade the National Association for the Welfare of Children in Hospital has built on these foundations, and now playgroup people (particularly those who had nursing experience in hospitals before acquiring playgroup experience later) are widening this much needed service.

Sometimes a space at the end of a ward, or in a side-ward, or on a covered balcony, is set aside as the playroom for mobile children; sometimes the activities are set up down the length of a ward, so that those in bed can see what is going on.

Children in hospital need an extension of the playgroup leader's understanding: often their concentration span is of short duration, and a child who usually enjoys complicated jigsaw puzzles may revert to simple ones; children may be weak, and need smaller dolls, lighter books, less complicated con-structional toys; they may be emotionally drained by the whole experience and need a chance to be soothed and comforted with little or no expenditure of effort. Such children often derive great comfort from manipulating lumps of dough (cleaner, softer, more yielding than clay or plasticine) or from painting (perfectly possible, given a bed easel, spill-proof paint pots and an absorbent protective cloth between the child and the easel).

Playgroup leaders should be prepared for the fact that some children need to play out fears or resentments: a loved bed-companion may suddenly become the object of ill-treatment,

47

for instance. This is one of the reasons for giving children in hospital a chance to play, and the child should not be made to feel guilty. It must be accepted that a succession of attractive rag dolls and teddies will come to grief in this way, and that more must be provided.

One constant factor to emerge from talking to those helping in hospital playgroups is the distress that is felt when watching some of the children grow progressively weaker and die. Those who were previously nurses may be a little more prepared since they first came face to face with death at a stage where they were not as vulnerable as some of the mothers who are meeting this situation for the first time. But they all find it very, very hard to take. They watch the child dying and project themselves into the feelings of the parents concerned and also face the fear 'What if it were our child?' Yet they have also been glad that they have stayed on in work that they have come to love, and know that they have grown in stature through facing such fundamental issues.

Two variations deserve mention, since there is a need for an extension of such facilities: playgroups for those children who accompany parents on a hospital visit, but are not allowed into the ward concerned (where this facility is not available parents have to take it in turn to sit with their child in the waiting room, while the other visits the patient; one branch of PPA was instrumental in raising enough money to start and staff such a playgroup); and playgroups for out-patients. It is exhausting for a parent trying to keep a young child amused during a wait that may last for hours; and it can be a damaging experience for the child whose feelings vary between boredom and apprehension.

FOSTER CHILDREN

Short-term foster children are likely to have had as much change of environment as they can accept, and it is unlikely that they would want to be introduced to yet another collection of people, in yet another strange place.

Long-term foster children have rather different needs. As the law stands at present the child may find himself in an emotionally charged environment.

Where it is known that the child is in such a state of insecurity and tension, it could possibly ease the situation if both the child and his foster mother were drawn into a playgroup. If they will attend together until the child is ready to be left on his own for an hour or two a few days each week, several things could happen: the foster mother could be drawn into a new circle of friends, who could offer her an outlet for her own tension. Equally, the child could be helped to gain enough independence to stay and play without her. He would also have the opportunity to relate to other adults, and come to feel less totally dependent upon his foster mother.

ONE-PARENT FAMILIES

Already playgroups are proving their worth here. Sometimes the child is illegitimate, and both he and his mother live with the maternal grandparents; sometimes the mother has left the father and child, and neighbours look after him; sometimes the parents are divorced, and whichever parent has custody of the child is likely to have to work full time; sometimes one of the parents is no longer living or is serving a prison sentence.

Neighbours and grandparents can be a great stand-by, but in either situation the constant presence of a young child may be a strain, to the detriment of both. There is ample evidence to suggest that the situation is greatly helped if a neighbour or grandparent can, together with the child, join a playgroup. These children need particular care during the settling-in period, for separation already holds fears, but once this period is safely bridged there is often a dramatic increase in the confidence and happiness of the child.

Where the one parent has to work full time the playgroup is still able to offer friendship and support in the evenings and at weekends. I have heard several tales of playgroup parents inviting both the child and his parent to spend the weekend with them. Or they will have the child for the weekend (when he is happy to stay) in order to give the parent a much-needed chance to sleep late or visit prison or have a day alone.

Sometimes the mother of a playgroup child dies and whichever playgroup family lives nearest tends to come to the rescue gladly. The child is left with them each morning, taken to playgroup, kept until bed-time; the widower is invited into supper each evening; his shopping, washing, cooking and cleaning are done for him.

The sympathetic wife responds to this practical need and fails to see where it is leading. The husband grows anxious about his wife's increasing fatigue, but does not like to say anything 'in case she takes it the wrong way', and the widower can become emotionally dependent upon the family. Help needs to be given carefully if the child and his father are to be set upon the road to a new family relationship based on their own home.

CHILDREN IN RESIDENTIAL CARE

As with the short-term foster children, those who will be in residential care only briefly will usually be more secure if they stay in their own environment, and enjoy the play facilities on the premises.

Children likely to be in care for longer periods have special needs which are difficult for the staff to meet. The staff have to be careful not to show favouritism, and this can lead to the children losing the feeling that they matter to any one person in particular. However well run, an institution is not as intimate as a home; with the best will in the world, it is difficult for the staff to find time for a leisurely conversation with an individual child.

Playgroups can help in two ways. Local mothers can collect some of the three- and four-year-olds and take them to join their playgroup. It is a change of scene, an outing, a chance to make new friends, discover new toys and activities, make new relationships with mother-figures. Friendships can lead to invitations to visit local homes, where the children can re-capture the feeling of a home and family. One of the tragedies of these children is that sometimes they are 'adopted' by visiting 'aunties' who make much of them for a while—and then forget to visit or take them out or send them cards.

In a playgroup setting the child does not become so emotionally dependent on any one mother; he can share his affection among them and visit their homes occasionally without being unsettled.

If there are no local playgroups it may be possible for visiting mothers to create a playgroup in the Home. The playroom will almost certainly be equipped and already in use, but the advent of mothers from outside could be a welcome change, bringing new faces, new names, new clothes to look at and touch, new stories to hear, new songs to sing. This situation may also lead to visits to local homes; and it would be 'safe' to love such regular visitors as the playleader and her helpers.

PART III ACCOMMODATION

There are now several playgroups involving mothers and children in temporary residential care, and there need to be more, for sometimes the period of care is over a year. The morale of the mothers can be very low, and in this distressed state of mind tensions mount as mothers try to share cookers and laundry facilities. Sometimes the mothers are poor managers, with little understanding of children even at the basic level of how to feed and clothe them; but sometimes circumstances have temporarily defeated people who are not fundamentally inadequate, and their fortitude and abilities need to be called into use, both for their own sakes and that of the community in which they find themselves.

Almost always an outside helper is needed to enthuse and guide the mothers into starting their own playgroup, and she may well have to run the play sessions herself to provide the continuity and the example of 'how it's done'.

Some of the mothers are so burdened by five children under five that all they ask is that two or three shall be removed for a few hours; sometimes they are eager for the stimulation of working with a lively adult who has the gift of making everybody feel wanted and needed; sometimes they enjoy learning new skills—one such derived great satisfaction from learning to crochet. Many of these mothers feel 'pushed around' and the last thing they want is people drafted in to make them more adequate; yet some have shown a real aptitude for learning when their interest was roused through friendly, informal contact.

These mothers love their children, but they are at such a low ebb that it would be unreasonable to expect them to feel concern

51

about their children's intellectual development. Concern for the children is the playgroup leader's personal problem in the early days, but as they adjust to a good play environment and become easier to manage, the mothers' interest is aroused. In a similar situation would we not clutch at anything that seemed to 'work' where handling children was concerned? One of the most noteworthy features of a good playgroup is the ability of the mother to respond to a good playgroup leader, and copy all that she says and does. And copying is sometimes the first step in real learning.

Chapter 3

Parent involvement

Parent involvement is one of the most significant and valuable developments to emerge from the playgroup movement, and it could be the greatest potential of the playgroups of the future. The benefit to both parents and children is already clearly apparent in new towns, overspill towns, council estates, private housing estates, high flats, racially-mixed areas and rural areas.

WHY DOES IT WORK?

Today's young parents are under tremendous pressures as television, films, magazines and advertising set unrealistic standards and expectations.

Many mothers are not much more than children themselves; many are strained by living with parents or in-laws, or lonely because they have moved away from their families; many can enjoy their first baby, but cannot cope at all once the second and subsequent babies arrive; many are so deprived themselves that their own needs conflict with the constant demands of a family.

Other mothers are able to cope more adequately, and they set their sights higher; they strive to 'live graciously', be Cordon Bleu cooks, have 'lively minds', and achieve bliss in bed. But now, with all the modern knowledge about the crucial importance of the first five years of life, society is in danger of making them feel that they are not good enough to bring up their own children. For many mothers, having a baby is the first time in their lives when they know the satisfaction of doing a job as well as anybody; this confidence needs to be reinforced *and used as a new growing point* if the gap is not to be widened between the parents and their children. There is a danger of children being increasingly ministered to by experts now that the crucial importance of these early years is recognized.

Playgroups offer the possibility of bringing together mothers and children, in order that they shall *both* have support and stimulation. Where a child has missed out it is often because his parents missed out before him, and they simply do not know what good parents should say, and do, and provide. During these years of talking with mothers in playgroups it has become quite clear to me that many mothers, once they see and hear what goes on in a good playgroup, can and do go home and start to put it into practice. It is not true that the mothers cannot and will not learn. On the contrary, all that many of them need is a living example to follow.

In other areas mothers may already be making a first-class job of bringing up their families but they, too, often derive great comfort and stimulus from being in the playgroup. Many of them set themselves such high standards that they feel strained and near breaking point; it is a relief to meet others in the same situation, and to discover that what seemed to be a unique and worrying problem is common to many mothers at this stage.

It is disturbing to find such a high incidence of maternal depression. The deliberately light-hearted query, 'Am I the only one who can remember real flashes of panic lest I was going round the bend?' brings forth a gale of laughter from open meetings, playgroup course sessions, or informal groups. It is not the laughter of amusement, but of relief at finding a hidden experience shared. People will come up afterwards or wait outside to say, 'You don't know what a relief it was to know that other people had been through it.'

Other mothers who benefit are those who feel frustrated in these child-bound years. A decade or so ago it was really not done for middle-class mothers to go out to work; now we have reached the stage where it is almost not done to stay at home.

Possibly the accepted knowledge that as much as fifty per cent of a child's intelligence is developed in the first four years of life will give these child-bound years a new status. Perhaps the monotony of the daily routine will slip into the background, compared with the creativity of laying the foundations of a unique human being. Meanwhile, it helps if those finding it more than difficult to adapt to a maternal role can share their frustration, and often their guilt. The playgroup and its allied activities offer a creative outlet that works wonders for their morale, and begins to give them back a feeling of identity.

Other mothers are lonely or shy, and the playgroup provides a neighbourhood meeting point. Again and again I hear that the first thing a couple do when they move to a new area is to get in touch with the nearest playgroup, 'and you've got friends at once, it's marvellous!'

The children need the presence of men in their predominantly feminine world, and more and more playgroup leaders are inviting men into the playgroups—policemen, firemen, milkmen, grandfathers, husbands on shiftwork. Saturday Fathers' Days are just beginning to catch on; the average man hates Saturday shopping, and husbands are beginning to discover that they can run a playgroup with a minimum of help while wives shop or cook.

But there are warning signs too. Sometimes husbands feel threatened as they see their wives begin to grow in stature, discovering resources within themselves about which they were previously unaware. If the husbands are also involved, then the growth is parallel. If they are not, then they can suffer severe loss of confidence; or, alternatively, they can (and do) assert themselves by refusing to allow their wives to continue, either with the playgroup or the playgroup courses.

HOW CAN IT BE ENCOURAGED?

It will spread only as people understand the need for it to do so. Often a playgroup leader on a course will say, 'We don't need mothers on a rota, we find we can manage better without them.' It comes as a surprise if the answer is 'I'm sure you can manage without them—but have you ever wondered if they can manage without you?' Once this idea has been introduced, mother-involvement sometimes follows.

Many playgroup leaders feel that they would like to try the idea, but do not know how to switch from one system to another. Sometimes a playgroup leader calls a meeting and puts it to the mothers, who are often caught up by her enthusiasm and respond gladly. Sometimes the beginning is more cautious; a start is made by a spontaneous act of kindness—a husband leaves home, a child dies, a demanding relative living at home reduces the young mother to tears of exasperation, and the playgroup leader says, 'Come and spend the morning with us.' And from this point on it can grow.

New groups often have no clear idea of how they want to organize themselves. If the parent co-operation system is explained they like the sound of it, and decide to start this way.

IS IT ALWAYS POSSIBLE?

No, not without more understanding and support than is available at the moment; some playgroup leaders are frightened of domination by the more aggressive mothers in their community and stirring speeches about the value of mother-involvement are useless. Regular supportive visits are needed at frequent intervals. In many areas the social services, educational and playgroup advisers work closely with the voluntary area organisers to try to ensure that each playgroup has the visits, and visitors, that it needs.

Some women are splendid with children but become self-conscious with other adults present and cannot face a rota system. Sometimes a playgroup leader discovers that she has no patience with adults, although she may be endlessly patient with children. Sometimes her own personality is such that other mothers find her difficult to get on with in other ways. Sometimes the mothers in a particular area do not respond to a particular playgroup leader who would be warmly welcomed elsewhere. Sometimes a playgroup leader finds that, willing as she is to try, the mothers just do not rise to responsibility. The worry of never knowing whether or not the rota mothers are going to turn up on their particular morning becomes too much, and three or four stalwarts decide to carry the playgroup between them.

Very occasionally participation is rendered virtually impossible by the requirements that every mother (even if she is only on the rota one or two mornings a term) must have a chest X-ray, and fill in a long and detailed medical form.[1] The X-ray

1 By 1976 it was generally accepted that full-time staff and helpers should be X-rayed initially and thereafter at 3-yearly intervals; infrequent helpers (e.g. one morning a fortnight) need not be X-rayed, provided that any persistent cough is promptly investigated, including an X-ray if indicated.

is no hardship in a town, or where a mobile van is available, but in some country districts the journey into the nearest town is long and expensive, with a young brood in tow. Sometimes the playgroup has different children on different days, and seventy mothers may apply for X-rays, only to be told that the hospital is unable to cope with this number. Sometimes private arrangements then have to be made, at a cost of up to £3·15. Other areas take the view that the regular playgroup leader and assistant must certainly be X-rayed, but that the infrequent mother-helper is no more of a hazard than the local shopkeeper or visiting friend.

The health forms deter for rather different reasons; some ask if there is any family history of mental illness, and both embarrassment and anxiety are aroused as mothers remember Uncle Herbert's suicide or old Aunt Jayne's spell in a psychiatric ward. Husbands sometimes refuse to co-operate, saying that this is an unwarranted intrusion into privacy, bearing in mind that a rota mother is at no time in charge of the children, and that she may only be with them for eight or nine hours a term.

Sometimes the struggle to explain, reason and coax on all sides grows too much for the playgroup leader, and she takes the easiest way out and abandons the idea of involving the parents. Surely this is a pity?

WHAT CONSTITUTES INVOLVEMENT?

No one running a valuable playgroup for children should feel inadequate or guilty about the fact that she is not also involving parents on a rota. Some involve parents in other ways. Some would now like to become a community playgroup but aren't sure if they could cope with the change-over, but to many the idea of having mothers in turn to be with the children throughout the morning is new and revolutionary, especially if they have been running private groups for many, many years, and they ask questions that need to be answered.

'Isn't there greater security for the children if I and my regular assistants are constant?' Possibly, but even an insecure child will find that two constant people give him the anchorage that he needs; the more confident ones begin to learn about adults

as a succession of 'extras' present themselves, one or two at a time, in their own secure playgroup world.

'*Is it fair for parents to pay, and then for them to have unskilled staff?*' It depends on what is understood by unskilled. Many mothers are highly gifted at story-telling, music, giving confidence and comfort to shy children, encouraging the diffident to talk, and the curious to discover. It is a question of discovering the strengths of the various mothers, and encouraging them to develop their gifts to the full. The security of the regular playgroup leader and her helper will provide the atmosphere of the playgroup, the mothers can be delightful extras.

'*Is it fair to ask the mothers to help; don't they need a rest from their children just for a few hours?*' Each mother's turn on the rota will only come round about every tenth playgroup day; if the playgroup only runs twice a week then she will only attend about twice a term.

'*If she comes so seldom is it worth coming at all?*' Yes, for the comment heard most often is 'It's lovely being with the children when you haven't got housework to bother about—somehow at home I always get on with the chores and never really see what she's doing at all.' It is this introduction of a mother to the world of children and their play that is so valuable. Also, for many mothers it is the first time they have had a chance to see just what sort of play material and books children enjoy.

One mother new to playgroup said, 'My little girl has asked if she can have a lump of your pink stuff for Christmas, where do you get it?' It was flour mixed with water and cochineal.

'*I like all my parents, but I just don't feel I could ever cope with them on a rota-system. I'm shy/bossy/prefer children to adults/haven't got any more nervous energy to spare. Short of a rota system, is there anything else that I can do to help?*' This playgroup leader is probably already offering her friendship, listening to their worries and sharing their interest in their children; she is probably also aware of the importance of the mothers staying with their children initially until the child is ready to stay alone in the playgroup.[1]

1 See Pre-school Playgroups Association leaflet 'Settling a Child into a Playgroup'.

Some may go on to arrange social evenings for the parents and see to it that newcomers are introduced to near neighbours and others; some arrange for speakers, or show films or film-strips about children; or encourage parents to arrange for private coaches or mini-buses to take them and their children to the sea, the zoo, the country or the pantomime.

Some have an eye for those who are lonely, and help them to feel wanted and needed by asking for help with such things as making dressing-up clothes, typing invitations or notices, washing the dolls' clothes, or repairing books. It is not a question of 'How can I get this done on the cheap?' but rather 'What pretext can I find for bringing parents into satisfying personal contact with us and each other?'

'Are we being asked to change the way we run our groups?' It is no good feeling that we 'ought' to change anything in response to pressure from outside. And no one should attempt to apply such pressure. No one should attempt to change for any reason other than a real desire to do so; and even when this desire is present it is still important to be aware of the difficulties.

For example, it is not easy to handle a child who is being 'difficult' when his mother is present, and when other mothers are watching; but if the playgroup leader can manage it in such a way that neither the child nor his mother feels that they have been disgraced, then the mother may have been given the insight and courage to take similar action at home.

Parent involvement offers a new dimension to working with children, and it would be quite unrealistic to suppose that all playgroup leaders are able to embark upon it—or even that they wish to do so. All good play provision for children should be welcomed; and all playgroup leaders should be credited with the desire to do as much for the children and their parents as they can do.

It should be clearly understood that many playgroups which do not have a mother-rota system *do* involve parents deeply, and their playgroup is the centre of real community action. Conversely, some playgroups boasting a compulsory rota system may have mothers feeling that they have been pressganged rather than involved. It is the quality of the involvement that matters.

Chapter 4

Standard, style and value

Most playgroup people warmly welcome visitors, especially those to whom they can turn for advice. Local playgroup advisers, nursery and infant advisers, health visitors, tutors, and above all, the voluntary area organizers of PPA visit by invitation (the latter extensively). The playgroups are all so different that the first year of visiting can be bewildering. Whatever our age or training we all tend to measure our first few playgroups by the nursery schools we have worked in, by our own playgroups, or by the first good playgroups we visited. All other playgroups are then compared with our original model, and we tend to pronounce judgment, and to arrange them mentally, 'A is better than B, but not as good as C.' It can take a long time for us to outgrow this judging attitude, but until we do we are not free to see each playgroup in its own unique setting.

POPULAR MISCONCEPTIONS

Many health visitors and social workers have proved to be of inestimable value to playgroups; their understanding that mothers as well as children have needs has enabled them to identify with the playgroup movement. The sensitivity that comes with years of visiting families in their homes is brought to bear as they begin to visit a wide variety of playgroups. Often their sound common sense, allied to good observation, enables them to be of real value to playgroups. But sometimes they misjudge the situation.

It is not unusual to hear 'Mrs X has hit upon such a splendid plan, she gives the children a good rush round when they arrive to let off steam, so that they'll settle quietly later on.' Others say, 'It's a pleasure to go into Mrs Y's group, all the children are

60

sitting around dear little tables, busy with their crayons and plasticine, and you could hear a pin drop.' The balance between mind and body is a delicate one at this age, and neither the letting-off steam nor the quiet-as-mice technique can achieve the balance required for really absorbed creative play.

Those of us who are nursery school teachers are not caught in these traps, but we can easily fall into others. We can remember our long ago, pre-war nurseries, where we all cleared away for milk and biscuits, and then had music and story time for everybody: some of us even remember expecting children to need the lavatory simultaneously; and when news-time was a must. We tend, at first, to approve of playgroups run on these lines, more than those run well on unstructured lines. Another trap into which we continually fall is overlooking the difference that mother-involvement makes to the situation, and in underestimating the complications caused by inadequate storage facilities. We may glibly say to a playgroup leader that the children must have books, forgetting that mothers who come from bookless homes will not see why; and that even if this is explained they still do not know *how* to introduce children to books; and if we do not show them what sort of books we are talking about, then the next visit may reveal a basket of books rescued from a jumble sale—the odd thriller and romance are left in for the benefit of the mother helpers, and the Girls' Annuals, Bumper Books and comics are presumed to have met the need we mentioned.

Similarly, we explain that children should put away one thing before getting out another. It comes back to us later, via the grapevine, that the X playgroup was furious and said, 'Doesn't she *know* that we don't have cupboards?' We had assumed (quite inaccurately and unreasonably) that the playgroup leader would have said to the other mothers, 'She says the children ought to get out, and put back, their own things: so as we haven't cupboards let's use that row of chairs as the depot for table toys during the play session; and the children can help us pack everything into the suitcases, lettuce crates, plastic laundry basket, hospital trolley or storage chest at the end of the session.'

Once we visitors have seen our own failures it becomes easier to re-examine what we had thought were the failures of the playgroups, and we come up against the problem of balancing standard with style and value.

STANDARD

In considering the range of equipment, activities, and child-adult relationships we should surely use the good nursery school as the ideal. With regard to the playgroup leader's relationship with the mother helpers, the comparison may be inadequate in certain respects. Yet it is still helpful to have an ideal at which to aim, especially as so many playgroups can and do reach an extremely high standard by using this model, and then working out for themselves the intricacies of this extra dimension occasioned by parent involvement.

Activities and equipment

Ideally, when the children arrive the room will be prepared, and the playgroup leader will be waiting at the door to greet the children.

Hall committees willing, and storage space permitting, the following activities will be awaiting the children—water play; wet and dry sand; clay and/or dough (as stuff to be manipulated); woodwork; painting; well-equipped home corner complete with dressing-up clothes, and possibly dough for 'cooking'; table toys; books; bricks; push and pull toys; large junk from which to make cars, boats, etc; climbing and balancing apparatus; and tables offering an inviting selection of odds and ends, glue, scissors, etc. which encourage children to experiment freely and imaginatively, in two or three dimensions, combining several skills. There will also be the means available by which children can discover various sounds for themselves before music becomes more formal.

A great deal of the child's experience of these activities will be undertaken alone, as deeply personal discovery and experiment. But in addition to this freedom-to-discover, there needs to be opportunity-to-share with other children and with adults. These experiences may include story-telling; music and movement; singing, rhymes, and fingerplays; the introduction of special interests such as flowers, leaves, fruit, vegetables, animals, insects, collections (such as bottles, in different shapes, sizes and colours; or a variety of different objects all of one colour); and conversation.

In spite of shortage of money, and difficulties over storage, it is impressive that so many playgroups reach such a high standard in all the above respects.

Management of activities and children

Naturally enough, it is more difficult to manage activities than to present them. It is also difficult to relate to children in a playgroup if you do not understand the real nature of play; or if you know your own child, without knowing too much about the needs of children in general, and three- and four-year-olds in particular. It is in this sphere that playgroup people need more help, for the standard of management usually falls below that of provision of play opportunities.

Most of the difficulty stems from the misinterpretation of free play, coupled with the fact that discipline seems to be a dirty word at present in our society. Free play is *not* the absence of any community rules, and a licence for all to do as they like. It means that the children are free to choose what they want to do; free to do it for as long as they like; and free to change their occupation when they wish. But they should not be free to pursue their own interests at the expense of other people. They should not be free to trail sand over the floor, because it would spoil the evening pleasure of the dancers or badminton players. They should not be free to scream, shout or make loud gun noises to the point where the other children suffer (literally suffer) from noise exhaustion. They should not be free to soak themselves, or others, at water play, for parents worry about taking children home in wet clothes. They should not be free to tear books, bite puzzles, or break toys, for then subsequent users suffer. For obvious reasons no one should be free to hurt any other child, animal or property. Only in this framework of community rules can any child truly be free to learn by doing.

Yet lack of the right sort of discipline is by no means the only threat to real free play. Through lack of understanding all too many playgroup leaders are inhibiting the innate creativity of children because they have not understood the link between learning and teaching. Frequently mothers will say to play-group leaders, 'Do they only play? I was hoping he'd learn something.' Or, 'Don't you teach them *anything*?' Or, 'My husband says it's silly to pay for her just to play about, we'd do better to spend the money to have her privately coached for the term before she goes to school.' Or, 'Well, I'd rather she went to Mrs X's playschool down the road, where she'll learn something.' The idea is firmly ingrained in most adults that one only learns if one is taught.

It is going to take great patience and skills, if we are to help people to understand that the experience of learning-to-learn has to be firmly established in a child before anyone should expect to teach him. And children can only accomplish this stage by being left free to repeat simple activities again and again and again. For example, one child spent weeks playing with wet sand, dry sand and water, not 'doing anything' just 'playing', but there came a day when she said, 'I like *that* sand (dry silver sand), it's all soft; and I like water, water's all soft, but the wet sand's all horrid between my fingers.' Why should two soft things mixed together not be soft? She was not ready to ask such a question, but by handling and observation she was already learning about the properties of sand and water, and was able to put some of her discoveries into words. This is learning-to-learn.

Playgroup leaders defeat the very thing they are trying to bring about if they teach children to make things before the children have had hours and hours of individual exploration in order to discover some of the properties of paper, paint, glue, clay, dough, wood, as 'stuff'.

Similarly, children are robbed of the chance to learn to make decisions for themselves if they are endlessly required to be pliable and responsive to orders. At first glance a playgroup may be most impressive; in a calm and peaceful atmosphere children are all busy, and the adult in charge may be delightful. Only slowly does one begin to register what is happening as one listens to the pleasant voice saying, 'Now, who hasn't made an ashtray for Daddy yet? Peter! Come on, there's a chair free now. Are you going to make a round one, or a square one?' 'John! You've had a long turn on that see-saw, what about Jane having a turn?' 'Sarah! What are you going to do? Would you like to play with the sand? No? Well what about the water? No? Well, we must do something, mustn't we?

Come on, you come with me and we'll look at a book.' In the nicest possible way she is organizing everyone, until in the end they sit or stand passively, waiting to be told what to do.

We mothers are all too apt to direct children: sit up straight; eat it slowly; you've had enough now; come in for tea; blow your nose; don't spill it; run out to play; put on your coat; take off your boots. On and on we go at home. What a tragedy if children continue to be subjected to this pattern at the playgroup! This might be the one place where a child can be certain that he is truly going to be free (within the limit of community rules) to *choose* what he wants do to; to *decide* what to do next. Choice and decision are part of learning-to-learn, even if there is a decision to do nothing for a while.

The management of 'difficult' children

Again, there is misunderstanding as people confuse a difficult child with a 'child that I find difficult to manage in the group'. Often there is confusion over what is naughty (deliberate) and what is an accident. It is important to be able to see the difference, for learning-to-learn includes making mistakes, being helped to put things right, and helped to understand what went wrong at a very simple practical level.

If the playgroup leader is cross over an accident, or if she copes alone with the aftermath, the child is denied the opportunity to learn from this mistake; and unless he is helped to understand and cope with a great many such accidents he will be unable to reach the stage of experience where he reacts with appropriate concern, but without crippling guilt.

So 'standard' relates to the provision of equipment and activities; to management of these activities; and to the relationships with individual children.

STYLE

The definition in this context is the plan, programme or time-management of the play session. There are two main styles, each firmly based on the idea of allowing children the maximum possible time to enjoy experimenting with the fullest possible range of activities. The difference between the two styles hinges on the word *possible*.

The unstructured session

Everything is available throughout the session. Milk or juice and a snack are quietly brought into the room almost as soon as the children are happily settled, and an adult is near at hand. Those children who eat poor breakfasts usually come and sit down at once, chatting easily with each other and the available mother. Other children are too absorbed to bother, and it is only as they flag that thoughts turn to elevenses. In this way, no serious play is interrupted, no world of make-believe is rudely shattered, no deep concentration is broken; for learning-to-learn is largely dependent on lengthening spans of concentration.

If there is an extra room available, an adult may walk towards it saying, 'I'm going to tell a story, would anyone like to come?' and those who wish to do so will follow her (thus the opportunity of free choice is offered to the children, to foster this learning-to-learn). Or a mother may sit in the book corner and gather a spontaneous group about her as she tells stories, or sings with them.

Music may happen in the same way. Sometimes almost all the children will join in; sometimes a few will want to watch, or others may prefer to continue with their self-imposed tasks. But no one is free to spoil music or a story that is giving joy to others; consideration for others will demand that he is offered another choice. 'Would you like to join us, or would you rather find something quieter to do?'

Sometimes parents say that they 'don't think children *should* do what they want all the time'. A well-run unstructured session is far from being undisciplined, for constantly the good of the community has to be safeguarded. Instead of saying, 'You must come and listen to the story', the playgroup leader is saying, 'I'm going to tell a story: come and listen if you like, or find something quieter to do—for you can't be noisy for the moment.' The children are learning the difficult art of self-discipline, which combines both obedience and choice—far, far more difficult than unquestioning obedience.

The three-part session

Usually the first hour-and-a-half is devoted to the free choice of a wide range of activities as before. Then the room is cleared, and tables and chairs are arranged in such a way that all can have elevenses together; this is turned into something of a ceremony, with children helping to set the tables, hand round the apples or biscuits and bottles or mugs of milk or juice. The adults usually sit with the children, who are encouraged to hold conversations and to tell their news. When everyone has finished then the room is cleared again for music and movement, or a story, or rhymes and fingerplay.

Which is best? There are so many variable factors that it's not easy to make a clear-cut choice.

Sometimes equipment has to be dismantled and carried outside to be packed into a very small storage shed. It takes time to unbolt a large climbing frame, and unless the biggest things are tackled by 11 a.m. it is impossible to have everything completely cleared and the children ready dressed by 11.45 in order that mothers may collect them and still meet the five-year-old at the school gate at dinner time.

Neither is every playgroup leader able to manage the session in such a way that self-discipline is evident throughout. And if she cannot, then the session can degenerate into a free-for-all. This becomes pointless for everybody, and exhausting into the bargain. But a playgroup leader who is not yet able to maintain this degree of unobtrusive control for three unbroken hours may be able to manage the three-part morning most successfully. In this case it is probably better to work within this framework that offers everyone greater security.

In some areas children never enjoy a family social meal. Sitting down together with an adult to eat and converse is an experience that some children may never have until they reach school—and not even then if the staff do not eat with them. Some playgroup leaders who know these families well and note that the children's concentration span at play tends to be short initially, feel that the age-old ritual of eating together to signify friendship is valuable.

Children are hungry for uninterrupted play experiences, hungry for relaxed conversation with adults, hungry for food, hungry for what lies behind the rituals that had their origin in deep human needs. It takes a sensitive and experienced playgroup leader to balance all the children's needs, her own strengths and weaknesses, and the limitations of her environment in such a way that she satisfies as many children as possible, as deeply as possible.

VALUE

Eventually most of us see enough of the two styles of running a playgroup to become aware that either may be good or poor— it all depends on the playgroup leader. We are left with the problem of wondering how to raise the standard of the poor groups.

But what is a poor group? Before making a comparative judgment we need to look closely at the environment.

We may be saddened to see children painting on small sheets of paper, with what looks like pale dishwater or coloured porridge: a glance out of the window may reveal back-to-back housing, or skyscraper flats, and we may decide that any sort of painting is better than none.

Standard is comparative. In some areas inadequate painting would be a retrograde step from the home environment; in others it offers wonders undreamed of. The field of comparison widens—'This isn't as good as it might be, but it is very much better than no playgroup at all.' After talking with the mothers involved it becomes clear that they are so much happier than they were before it started, and one feels that home must be a very much happier place too.

Care is needed at this point, lest the present good is lost in our stampede to make it better. A willingness to change must precede any changes, and this attitude can only come about in a relationship of mutual affection and respect. The mothers, too, will be learning-to-learn, and nothing succeeds like success. One such group was fostered in a mining village by an experienced member of PPA; no books were available, so she took along some of her own children's books; they remained unopened and neglected in a corner for weeks on end; she dropped in, in a friendly fashion, several times and stayed for coffee and a chat; one day she took her coffee to the book corner, and opened one as she drank; children gathered round— but a couple of minutes was the limit of their concentration span. Weeks went by, and the pattern was repeated regularly with growing enjoyment each time. When she had to miss a few weeks, she asked the local Infants Head to drop in, just to keep up the enthusiasm and morale of the mothers. On her first visit the head said 'Do you read stories to the children?' and there was a chorus of 'yes' from mothers who had never been known to go near the book corner. But from then on whenever their first visitor popped in there was almost always a different mother looking at books, or telling stories with a group of children.

The greater the value of a playgroup in its particular community the more careful we must be in our attempts to raise its standards.

When visiting a playgroup the question in one's mind should not be 'How does the standard of play here compare with that of a good nursery school?', but rather 'What is happening here and in the homes of these children, as a direct result of the playgroup?' If the answer to this second question is that the children are having more stimulation and a greater range of experience than they formerly had, and if the mothers are happier, less anxious and guilt-ridden and more enlightened than they were—and if the husband is aware of increasing harmony all round—then it is a good playgroup. And patient, kindly, helpful visiting may make it a very good playgroup indeed.

WHO CAN HELP?

From the early days of the Pre-school Playgroups Association the voluntary area organizers have been the backbone of the movement: it is they who are constantly available with practical help and advice; who will take new enthusiasts to see established groups and put them in touch with playgroup courses; who will contact isolated groups to say 'If you want me, I'm here.' This invitation is usually accepted with alacrity, and a supportive bond of friendship is formed. The aftermath of a first visit is clearly predictable: when a query arises the immediate reaction of the playgroup leader is to ring up her area organizer. This is often accompanied by a request for another visit. This is difficult to refuse, especially as experience shows so clearly that it is much easier to prevent a playgroup 'going wrong' in these early stages than it is to wait until it is too late and then try to put it right.

Once this relationship is established the wear and tear on area organizers and branch committee members is heavy. The telephone rings incessantly, and people in need can be extraordinarily thoughtless. They phone NOW, in the middle of Sunday lunch, at children's bath-time, during the breakfast rush hour, and even when husbands and wives are asleep. The really wearing phone calls are those prompted by upsets: a parent has turned nasty, a child had an accident (very rare, this) and the playgroup leader feels guilty even though it was not her fault; the village hall committee has put up the rent; the promised hall has been snatched away, just when they thought they had it; the treasurer has just gone off with the money ('No, we weren't insured'); one partner leaves the group and takes the equipment with her ('No, we didn't have a constitution'); a playgroup wife is nearly demented because her husband has left her; a mother is distraught because her child has been killed in an accident; the new playgroup leader is a disaster ('How can we get rid of her? She's very well known locally'); a mother is being awful to her child, and the playgroup leader is sure he'll be ruined for life if she does nothing—but what? The PPA representative listens, and listens, and listens, until she feels wrung out, for she listens with her heart as well as her head.

Who else has the degree of caring or the time to listen like this? Isn't this what society needs? PPA is answering this need quietly and unobtrusively, and at great personal cost, for few listeners feel confidently equipped for the task. They fear to say the wrong thing, and they live through a great deal of real anguish before they discover that the talker hardly ever asks for advice, let alone direction; the need is for a willing, unjudging, understanding listener and at long last the talker says, 'I'm sorry I've bothered you like this, but I feel ever so much better now that I've talked to you.'

This chain of help is passed on, for these same playgroup leaders are, in turn, phoned up by the mothers of the playgroup children. The causes of distress are a different set of problems, but equally predictable: the child has enjoyed playgroup right from the very first day but now he has suddenly gone off it;

'Herbert's turned really nasty to the baby'; 'Ann is so clinging when I'm on rota duty that I feel awful'; 'Jane shows off so badly when I'm on rota duty that I feel awful'; 'Peter can't understand why I don't do my rota duty now that the baby's so nearly due, and *he* feels awful'; 'Now that I'm at home alone with the new baby, and I don't see you all, *I* feel awful.'

The real cause of distress is the child's difficulty in learning to share his mother. The playgroup does not cause these problems but allows the manifestations to appear, and once the signs are there the mothers who have been through that stage can rally round with reassurance. The stream of anxieties continues: 'My husband gets so impatient when Dean wants the landing light on, but he gets so frightened with it off'; 'The big ones are so bossy with Lynne, and it seems to be rows all the time'; 'Our Pat's black and blue where William pinches her in the playgroup, and my husband says he isn't going to stand for it'; 'Alec had a new white jersey on this morning, and it's ruined with red paint on the sleeves'; 'Jenny's not to do music any more, her knickers are filthy from that floor'; 'Amanda used to paint ever so nicely at home, and now she only paints these messes'.

They are all such little problems set down on paper, but they loom so large when you are at home alone all day—babies and monotonous jobs such as washing-up, bed-making, preparing food and cleaning leave the mind wide open for turmoil to develop over any one of these matters.

In other areas it is the shoe leather that is worn, for mothers here do not remember where the nearest telephone box is situated, and they are afraid to use it if they do. The popping-in technique has to replace the phone, and the problems are different again. 'You know you said to get a supervisor? Well, we've got her, she was a supervisor in the factory over the way'; 'Mrs X keeps sending Martin with chocolate wafers for lunch and the other kids whine because they haven't got any'; 'We've saved up £30 for a trip to the seaside, and now the Y playgroup says it's a waste and we ought to buy something for the playgroup, and we don't see why we should'; 'We'll never be able to buy a climbing frame, the Christmas party alone took £17'; 'Tracey's mother throws her weight about just because she's had seven kids of her own, and they're nothing to write home about anyway'; 'Bill's mother shouts at the kids so, and smacks them too; We all smack our own at home, but you shouldn't do it here should you?—it frightens the others'; 'What can we do about mothers who smoke all the time? It doesn't seem right to lean over the children and spill ash all over them.'

Area organisers learn to answer their *questioners*, not merely the questions. The 'sensible' comment on £30 for an outing might be 'Don't. The children need a climbing frame.' The sensitive comment is likely to be different. Parents want, and need, to pass on to their children, the high-spots of their own childhood, and Sunday-school outings to the sea-side rank high in our cultural heritage—to break the continuity of family experience can be as damaging in some respects as it is desirable in others. The cycle of enrichment is as valid as the cycle of deprivation. Wise befrienders know that memories and experiences shared and discussed can lead to new learning, growth and development—next year the group may still want to repeat a richly satisfying experience—but when the climbing frame eventually arrives it will be as the result of a new stage in the growth of the parents' observations and understanding, and the children will benefit even more from this than from the climbing frame.

Area organisers are the top-line volunteers of the playgroup movement: their knowledge and experience is shaping the nature and extent of the training for which they ask.

Since 1970 PPA has been holding Training Days nationally, regionally and locally—in some areas on-going groups are established and help many area organisers to extend their role to tutoring playgroup courses, and/or to running workshops and discussions for those not involved in playgroups but who are anxious to know how they can combine children and chores at home to the benefit of all concerned. Many area organisers are now forming teams of playgroup visitors, both to spread the workload, and to encourage experienced playgroup people to accept a new stage of responsibility, growth and learning.

What is the future for these able and experienced volunteers? The area organisers will continue to be needed, not only for the work they do but as the link between the playgroups and the many professionals now sharing responsibility for the under-fives and their families.

PPA can produce and train its volunteers, but *they cannot continue work on the scale needed unless local authorities can pay realistic expenses, especially in rural areas.*

Part II

Starting Playgroups

Chapter 5

What's in a name?

Nursery schools, day nurseries, nursery classes, playgroups, playschools, nursery groups, toddlers' groups, child minders, crèches: how are parents to know which to choose? Legal definitions and common usage have made it impossible to define all these terms accurately. The following attempt to clarify them can only be a guide, since there is considerable overlap and variation, especially in the voluntary and private enterprises.

NURSERY SCHOOLS

It would help to remove much damaging misunderstanding if this term were used only for those establishments run by education authorities. It could then rightly be assumed that they were free; that they were run by a teacher who had had three years' nursery school training (or, in Scotland, by a fully-trained teacher who had undertaken an additional year's training for nursery school teaching); that two-year trained nursery nurses (NNEB) were her assistants; that the premises and garden (which is obligatory) conformed to the standards required by the Education Act; that they operated for the same hours as the local schools; and that the age range was two to five years.

These state nursery schools are free to all children, and it is left to the head teacher to decide how she fills the places from her vast waiting list. In some counties there are no nursery schools at all, in others there are only one or two, so it is not surprising to learn that waiting lists can have over 1000 names on them. In some cases waiting lists are closed at a realistic level; heads anxious to have a full picture of local demand may keep the list open for their own interest, but they are careful not to raise the hopes of mothers who can have no hope of placing a child before school.

During the last three years, when speaking with heads of nursery schools, it is noticeable that they tend to tackle their waiting lists in one of two ways. They may give priority to children referred as being in actual need, or at risk. This can mean that there is not a single 'ordinary' applicant among the children. This is an unsatisfactory state of affairs since nursery schools aim to have a well-balanced cross-section of the community, where the less privileged child is helped by the more privileged child, and vice versa. In every case the head teacher has been troubled but has decided that her staff is strong enough to work with her to achieve the apparently impossible goal of readiness to go on to 'big school'. As they usually express it, 'If they start infant school with a backlog of five years of poor experience, and even poorer handling, what chance have they got?'

They may carefully keep a balance between privileged, under-privileged, handicapped, maladjusted and so-called average children.

This is not easy, and head teachers have harrowing tales to tell of deputations of mothers coming to say, 'It isn't fair to have children who live in nice houses with gardens, when you won't take some of the kids down our way who need it more.' In one case I was told of some mothers who withdrew their children, because they felt so guilty at taking the places of more needy children.

In order to give a chance to as many children as possible, many nursery schools make provision for children to attend either full time, or for part of a day.

State provision needs to be greatly increased if nursery schools are to achieve the balance of normality that is their greatest strength. And is not every child worthy of being helped towards the fullest possible version of himself?[1]

NURSERY CLASSES

These are attached to infant schools, under the infant head teacher. The running of the class is, ideally, undertaken by a

[1] In 1972 a White Paper, 'Education: A Framework for Expansion' opened the way for an increase in pre-school provision, including playgroups.

nursery school teacher, but this is not always possible in such a time of shortage.

From the children's point of view the difference between the two state systems is that in a nursery class they are living on the fringe of someone else's world; in a nursery school they are becoming masters of their own.

DAY NURSERIES

These come under the Social Services Department. They are open during working hours, and priority is given to the children of mothers who are the sole breadwinners, or to those whose social need is grave.

While nursery schools are free, a charge is made for a place at a day nursery: it varies over the country, and each area has its own sliding scale of charges according to the means of the applicants. The children range in age from a few weeks to five years. The matron in charge should be a trained nurse, or nursery nurse, with previous experience of normal children and a prior appointment as a deputy matron. The programme of play, and the care of the play equipment for all the age groups, should be the responsibility of an experienced nursery nurse, who has received additional training for the post.

The assistants in closest contact with the children are nursery nurses, or three students still in training may be counted as one trained nurse if the day nursery is used as a training centre. Extra assistants must be over eighteen years of age, and should have had in-service training after a short introductory spell in the day nursery.

There are private day nurseries, which have to meet the same requirements with regard to premises and staff, but their charges vary more widely. In one town, two private day nurseries in the same road charged £3·50 and £7 respectively for a five-day week, and the latter charge was not inclusive of breakfast. The play facilities vary considerably.

CHILD MINDERS

Officially, anyone taking into her home one child or more (who is not related to her) for two or more hours a day, for reward,

79

is a child minder. All such persons are required to be registered by the Social Services Department. House playgroups are child minders by this definition, and they are of varying quality.

MOTHER AND TODDLER CLUBS

There are many variations on this theme, but one particular pattern is beginning to spread slowly over the country, and it is of such value that I propose to describe this version only under the above title.

At their best, these clubs are intended for mothers—often in deprived areas—accompanied by their toddlers (loosely, children between the ages of about eighteen months and three). They may be initiated by a health visitor, social worker, play-group leader or other mature person who understands that the great need at this stage is for mothers to come together, *with their children*, in order that they may be reassured.

Few mothers are prepared for the developments of this second year of life. Often they have stopped attending the clinic, so no one is able to say, 'Look, you've got a beautiful baby—happy, healthy, secure, intelligent. And precisely *because* he is all these things he will soon begin to find his own personality, and to test both you and himself as far as he can go. Do not worry or get upset, you have not "done anything" or "gone wrong". But it can be a bit wearing, and a bit tricky domestically sometimes. Why not join our Toddlers' Club?' Often a playgroup will offer its equipment, and even playgroup leader, for an afternoon so that the mothers can relax together at one end of the hall, while the children investigate the toys and each other in the same room. There is great relief in comparing notes with other mothers at this stage; and even greater benefit if there is someone knowledgeable enough to listen to them and encourage discussions in which the mothers are able to discover some of the answers to their own problems.

The mothers can relax, seeing that the children are safe and happily absorbed; if a child is tearful or fearful his mother is at hand, and often he is perfectly contented to sit peacefully on her lap and watch the other children. Most mothers agree that one of the major causes of their exhaustion at this stage is the fact that they must watch and listen without a break for every waking minute of every day (and quite often during the night as well). A certain temperament of toddler at a certain stage literally makes it impossible for a mother to be alone even in the lavatory. This is the stage when some children can move and climb with great speed; and do not yet know the meaning of such words as sharp, hot, heavy, hard, fall, crush, dangerous.

Naturally enough, the longing of many of these mothers is to find a safe and happy place for the child where he can be left for a short while every day—hence the constant appeal to playgroups to admit two-year-olds. It is not lack of sympathy that prompts the Pre-school Playgroups Association to reiterate constantly that playgroups are intended primarily for the three- and four-year-olds. It is an awareness of two needs.

It is impossible to ignore all the weight of research pointing to the fact that the separation of mother and child should be gradual and confident; and that most children need to be with their mothers until they are three. The pattern of the Mother and Toddler Clubs allows the best of both worlds; the mother feels relaxed and is resting physically whilst being happily stimulated and reassured; the child is learning to explore a large room, new toys and activities, and other children on his own—yet within sight of the mother on whom he is still so naturally dependent.

Whether or not they acknowledge the fact consciously, the real fear of many mothers at this stage is that they are failures since their children are sometimes already beyond their control. They do not just want to dump-and-run; they long to put the child somewhere where 'they' will 'get him right again'. The urgent need at this crisis point is for the mother to be understood, accepted, *and helped to understand and manage her own child.*

CRÈCHES

This used to be the old name for what are now known as day nurseries, but today the term is widely and loosely used. In many cases so-called toddlers' clubs now come within this category.

If the crèche runs for less than two consecutive hours, and if no charge is made, then the venture does not have to be registered neither are the premises inspected. Some crèches give no cause for concern, even if they are not always as valuable as they might be for the children.

The term can cover a multitude of circumstances, however, and it conjures up an impression of children left with a band of volunteers to play together, while the mothers do the weekly shopping, attend church, or just have a morning free for appointments with doctors, dentists, hospitals or hairdressers. In theory, the idea is a good one. Few children enjoy being trailed round large stores; prams may have to be left outside, and often the baby is too heavy to be carried up to and around the various departments; but in practice, it may be less than ideal as children are left with complete strangers, often with no period of settling-in by the harassed mother concerned. Also the age range may vary from babies in prams to rising fives, and the noise and confusion may be considerable. On the other hand they can be excellent.

One such has been running for many years in a Salvation Army hall, adjacent to a market and shopping centre. It is open every day, with the same friendly, capable woman and her assistants, and the same wide range of activities awaiting the children. Many of the children attend regularly, and the settled atmosphere is such that the majority of new visitors are prepared to be left when the mothers say, 'Would you like to stay here while I do the shopping?'

One weakness of crèches tends to be that the willing volunteers are unable to provide sufficient equipment and activities to hold the children's interest; the age range is such that the little ones interfere with the play of the bigger ones, and are at risk physically during the process. Another is that there is often a lack of continuity in the voluntary helpers so that the children are unable to build a relationship with one well-known person; this is particularly distressing for some children.

PLAYGROUPS, PLAYSCHOOLS, NURSERY GROUPS

These are all personally chosen names, and convey nothing specific at all; it is quite impossible to choose between the groups merely on the basis of their names. All that can be taken for granted is that the premises and playgroup leaders have been passed by the Social Services Department; that the ratio of adults to children has been fixed officially and, in some areas, that the groups have not been allowed to start unless the playgroup leader is 'suitably qualified'. (See section on *Playgroup Leaders*, page 94.)

In theory, all those who start playgroups aim to give the children the richest play experience possible. The tremendous range of types and standards is due largely to the range of personalities of the playgroup leaders, and of their understanding of children, childhood, and the needs and strengths of parents.

For those new to the subject it may be helpful to oversimplify the situation, and to say that playgroups may be 'good', or 'rigid', or 'uncontrolled', and to clarify each category.

The good playgroup

A good playgroup provides a first-class environment where, in a happy, busy atmosphere, children are painting; experimenting with wet and dry sand, water, clay, dough, bricks, woodwork, climbing apparatus and a wide variety of table toys; playing imaginatively in the home corner, or on improvised ships and buses; listening to stories; looking at books; enjoying music; singing; or chatting with interested adults about anything and everything. There will be ample opportunity for the children to respond to beauty in many forms; they will be stimulated to curiosity, wonder, reflection, discovery and the excitement of discovering, thinking and planning. There will be the security that comes from community rules, kept out of consideration for others, and in this security the children will know freedom-with-responsibility.

Parents will know themselves to be wanted, needed and appreciated. They will rejoice in discovering and offering their talents, and in shouldering responsibility. There will be opportunities to be with, and learn from, the children and each other.

The uncontrolled playgroup

Usually those running such groups have enough learning to be familiar with the term 'free play', but not enough experience or understanding to know that children can only be free when certain community rules are obeyed. These groups run (and

83

that is the operative word) on a free-for-all system, and so much of the playgroup leaders' physical and nervous energy is spent in keeping a slightly fearful eye on the most aggressive or exuberant children that they completely fail to see that the timid ones are never free to do anything wholeheartedly: they live in perpetual anxiety lest they should be knocked over or shouted at; and the noise level exhausts them.

The rigid playgroup

These are more difficult to explain and understand, for the children often appear to be happy. The majority of parents have no hesitation at home in deciding when a child is happy-doing-the-right-thing or happy-doing-the-wrong-thing. However 'happy' William may be as he picks the heads off the tulips, he is diverted smartly to a more appropriate activity. But play and child development are so little understood by many parents that they have no such clear idea of what constitutes being happy doing the 'right' thing, or happy doing the 'wrong' thing in a playgroup.

In a rigid playgroup the children's activities are often controlled in groups, and even timed by the clock. For example, when they arrive they may each be given a small board and a ball of plasticine for the first twenty minutes. This may then be put away, to be replaced by shapes drawn on small pieces of paper and tins of wax crayons; the children are required to colour the shapes without going over the lines. This may be followed by a period of looking at books (given out, not chosen), and playing with table toys (also given out, not chosen).

Milk time may even be silent, with every child required to sit still until the slowest child has finished. The story or music time that follows may well be obligatory, and no allowance is made for those who are not able yet to concentrate for the span of a story, or those who would like to watch and listen to the music but feel unready to take an active part.

Many playgroup leaders from such groups attend playgroup courses, and listen with interest to modern methods, but are unwilling or unable to change their ways. Sometimes it is because of their insecurity, and many will say, 'I wouldn't like to change, the children never get out-of-hand this way'; or 'But our way is so much easier!' or 'I never could stand noise and muddle, this way suits me best.' But not all are like this.

Fortunately, in many cases the women running some of these old-fashioned groups radiate a brand of child-magic that speaks for itself; if their methods are old-fashioned so is their sound common sense, their particular brand of love, and their fund of real wisdom. One such claims an infallible cure for small boys frightened of the barbers; 'I just sit down on one of their little chairs, let him wrap a sheet round me, and cut *my* hair—it never fails.' Children in the care of such people gain a sense of security that is invaluable, but the needs of children are infinitely variable from child to child and day to day, and the more flexible the regime the more their needs will be met.

It is regrettable that these rigid playgroups so often call themselves nursery schools.

Chapter 6

How are playgroups started?

These are by no means the second-best form of playgroups; they exist in their own right and feel quite different from the larger groups in halls.

The variation is wide, but all the following may be considered to be typical:

Farm houses, where from four to fourteen or so children may gather together several times a week. Pet lambs, goats, calves, donkeys or ponies may be part of the playgroup scene. There are expeditions to gather eggs, blackberries, apples or frog-spawn; and adults who share the new experiences and talk about them. The joys of the country can be seen, heard, felt, smelt, tasted and stored up within.

Small terrace houses, holding perhaps up to six children, spread happily throughout the hall, kitchen and living room. They may paint in the kitchen, play with water at the sink, use the space under the stairs as a 'home', have bricks in the hall and table toys in the living room. One such playgroup stands out in my memory; no pains had been spared to turn it into a haven for children whose need was great; even the piano had been painted spindleberry pink. No wonder an appreciative fisherman father had made a special visit to say, 'Thank you, missus, you've done our Debbie a bloody bomb!'

Houses so spacious that it is possible to give the playgroup two or three rooms, where everything can remain in position for the next session. These groups may cater for as many as twenty children at a time.

The particular strength of housegroups lies in the feeling of home from home that some children need before they are ready to enter a bigger community. The smaller groups often have a

86

specific value, such as helping a child from another country to gain a second language, for there are fewer children's names to remember, closer friendships with fewer people, more familiar objects to identify and name, and a feeling of greater intimacy to set the scene for the sharing of new words.

Frequently husbands have made cupboards, shelves, outdoor equipment. One converted a garage with sand troughs attached to the back walls, easels and a large Wendy House attached to the side walls, and a carpet put down to cover the concrete floor. Each night the carpet was covered with sheeting before the car was carefully inched-in.

Is it surprising that such husbands and wives think in terms of 'our playgroup'? Committees would be out of place as they work out for themselves what they would like to do next for the children in their home and garden. It is not at all unusual for such groups merely to break even, or even to run at a slight loss. Several husbands explained it by saying, 'My wife doesn't smoke, and hardly ever drinks, and she gets a terrific kick out of doing this, so I'm prepared to call her loss her cigarette money.'

The community must be very careful not to judge and condemn all private groups as profit-making groups. Many are truly charitable in a moral sense, but cannot be registered as charities without a committee and constitution. At the moment such house groups are not eligible for grants (in the few cases where grants are given) because they are deemed to be profit making. It would help if such cases could be judged on their merits, for many are serving needy children who can afford to pay so little that endless fund-raising activities are necessary in order that adequate equipment may be bought and made.

One mother announced with regret that the playgroup would have to be stopped for a term as she was due to have a major operation. The other mothers said, 'Why can't we carry on for you? We've hung around here in your hall chatting, and we know exactly what to do, and where things go, and we could keep the house ticking over for you too.' So they did, for the whole term, with washing-up, bed-making, and a spot of cooking thrown in.

The above types of group need cause no concern, but others give just cause for disquiet. Some people are undoubtedly

87

jumping on the band-wagon, spurred on occasionally by an article in a glossy magazine suggesting that 'playgroups can be run for pin money'. If they are started for this motive there is the temptation to charge too much, and to provide too little equipment. Such playgroups can be a very limiting experience, where children may be given nothing more inspiring to do than thumb through piles of indifferent books, and play with cardboard cartons filled with a miscellaneous selection of other people's cast-off toys.

HALL GROUPS

Private enterprises

Some people need to earn a salary according to their professional scale. One nursery school trained teacher said, 'This is my profession. I have got to help my husband with our mortgage. I can't work in a nursery school because there isn't one, and teaching the over-fives just isn't my cup of tea. Yet I'm made to feel guilty at earning money doing a worthwhile job well! Would people really rather that I went to work in a shop, which is the only other job I'd be likely to get?'

Others, sometimes with fewer qualifications, may need to earn a modest but adequate salary and if they offer the children a really worthwhile experience, and the parents choose to pay accordingly for this service, then this is a personal decision that no one has the right to question.

The groups that should concern everyone are those where the motive to make money is very much stronger than the desire to help the children, or where the desire to help the children is real enough, but the knowledge of how to do so is lacking.

In one such group the mothers paid 25p a morning, and the children ran round pushing chairs, climbed on the table and jumped off, or looked at piles of tatty comics. Such people usually start with the best possible motives, but know so little about children, childhood and play that the group is almost bound to be very poor indeed. If they have no committee, and no mothers are involved, only the playgroup leader and her assistant may know what goes on. It may be a very long while before parents discover that all is not well with the playgroup, for they tend to assume that, if their child is not happy, there must be something wrong with *him*. One such child was entered for a playgroup, and on being asked in a friendly fashion if he liked playing with other children, a heavy silence engulfed the three. Then the mother said diffidently, 'I suppose I ought to tell you, he was expelled from his first playgroup. Will it make any difference?' The playgroup leader assured her that it would not, and the mother went on, 'He was only three at the time, but he was expelled at the end of the first week because he wouldn't concentrate, or co-operate—they said that he wouldn't even try to write his name.' No playgroup, run by either trained or untrained playgroup leaders, should attempt any such kind of formal work.

Parent involvement as rota helpers tends to be less in profit-making groups, partly because those who start them usually say that they can manage without parents (and they have not understood that many parents *need* to be involved) but more often because they are fair-minded and say, 'I charge more than many groups, and I think that if parents are paying for the best they have the right to expect a constant and able staff; certainly they shouldn't be expected both to pay *and* work.' Yet many of these playgroup leaders go to great lengths to establish a warm personal relationship with their mothers. Many arrange social events, talks, holiday outings, and even organize coach or van parties to attend playgroup courses if word gets around that 'they are ever so helpful for just mothers as well as playgroup leaders'.

Community playgroups

There are several variations on this theme.

1. The most usual way of starting is for a group of friends and neighbours to decide that they need a playgroup. In more privileged areas this need is felt spontaneously, and the idea spreads rapidly by word of mouth, telephone, or an advertisement in the local paper. A meeting follows, permission is sought from the social services, there is usually a request to the Pre-school Playgroups Association for guidance, the relevant publications are purchased, a committee is elected, and a constitution is drawn up to give charitable status.

In less privileged areas the need is usually sensed by a few only, and it may take very much longer to cover the same ground; but if these few take all the initiative and keep it, the parents whose need is greatest are not nursed over their apathy-barrier, and the project does not engender the fire of enthusiasm necessary to launch the playgroup safely.

2. A playgroup may be started off by an existing group of women, such as the Young Wives, the Mothers' Union, the Women's Institute, or the Townswomen's Guild. A Committee is formed; a charitable status constitution is drawn up and the whole group sets to work to raise money and collect equipment. The mothers of the playgroup children may form the committee, provide the playgroup leader, and supply the helper-mothers. Everything is decided democratically, and any money over after paying the rent and the playgroup leader is ploughed back into the playgroup in the form of equipment.

3. An existing group may sponsor a playgroup, but decide that they do not wish to be involved in the actual running of it. They provide the committee, which appoints the playgroup leader, raises the funds, and allocates the spending money. But the playgroup leader runs the playgroup.

Sometimes a committee member is present each day, ostensibly to collect the money, but really to be available to chat with anyone who needs it—this leaves the playgroup leader free to devote herself to the children.

Occasionally, there is too little liaison between the committee and the playgroup leader, who may find that unsuitable equipment has been provided without reference to the present needs of the children. But usually she is well content to devote herself to the children and mothers in the knowledge that all the administrative jobs are being undertaken by others.

4. The 'every-mother-a-leader' group. These flourish well in areas where money is so tight that there is no hope of any mother being able to pay more than 5p or 8p for a morning's play. Even if the rent is nominal, clearly there is nothing over with which to pay a playgroup leader even a token salary. Mothers in this situation need someone to start them off, and to remain on call afterwards. It may be a vicar, or minister, a

children's officer, a social worker, or a mature member of a voluntary association such as an area organizer of PPA. The mothers then take it in turn to provide daily groups of playgroup leaders. Variations on this theme were dealt with in Chapter 1.

It is advisable for playgroups to register as a charity when their constitution is in order;[1] it is regretted that so many groups do not understand the practicalities of charitable status and deliberately refrain from seeking it, in the mistaken belief that the playgroup leader will not be allowed to receive payment, neither will the playgroup be able to put away a small sum for emergencies.

Charitable status indicates to the community that the playgroup committee has a responsible attitude to finance, but is not run for financial gain. Playgroups not registered as charities, even if they are not making a profit, may find that they are not eligible for grants from various sources.

5. The playgroup coaxed into existence unobtrusively by an authority employee, or a voluntary worker. The method may vary from knocking on doors to putting up notices in clinics and shops or slipping invitations to a meeting through 2,000 letter-boxes (a 1 per cent response is usual, but it is enough).

The catalyst continues to lead from the rear and to offer 'training' disguised as 'meetings'. Six to nine valuable learning-packed months may well precede the opening of the playgroup, and those impatient for the children's sake must understand that during this period the children are benefiting at home through their mothers' increased happiness and learning.

6. Mother and Toddler Clubs often produce a few mothers who decide that they want to start a playgroup for the three-year-olds who have outgrown the all-mothers-and-toddlers-together stage, and who need a fuller range of equipment. These mothers are used to being in a group and often have the confidence and incentive to attend a local playgroup course. If they are not yet ready for this, they are ready and willing to attend workshop sessions and discussions with a playgroup adviser, tutor or area organiser in their familiar hall.

[1] See PPA publication 'The Business Side of Playgroups'.

Chapter 7

Playgroup premises

The approval of the premises rests with the local Social Services Department, and the ruling is laid down so clearly in the Nurseries and Child Minders Act that there is no need to reproduce it here. But there is a real need to bring the picture to life.

STORAGE SPACE

This is the most pressing problem of all for many playgroup people. The following storage facilities are not unusual.

The space under stages. Sometimes this involves carrying everything (including sand) up and down a six-rung ladder; sometimes it involves creeping through a door two feet high, and moving in on all fours to make room for everything.
Lofts. Not always with a solid permanent ladder.
Basement or cellars. Often these are damp, which means that dressing-up clothes etc. must be kept in plastic sacks or taken home during the holidays. Ladders without handrails, or worn steps, add to the difficulties.
Out-houses. These vary widely, but I have seen the following: disused stables, a garage on the opposite side of the main road (which had to be crossed with every single piece of equipment at the height of the morning rush-hour, and again during the lunch-hour rush) and a never-ending selection of wooden sheds bought and erected by the parents with the proceeds of countless coffee mornings and jumble sales.
Cupboards and store-rooms. These are rarely big enough, and there is nowhere for big equipment (except when the hall is

92

particularly high, and then it is not unusual for a metal climbing frame to be hoisted aloft with pulleys, out of the way of the badminton players, and secured by nylon ropes). Often the storage space is shared by others, and there are sad tales of damage and loss. Sometimes the position is so confusing that playgroup toys and small equipment are accidentally sold at other people's jumble sales.

Often permission to buy or build cupboards is turned down by hall committees; sometimes because it is considered that there is not enough room, but sometimes because it would 'spoil the appearance of the hall'. Incredibly, quite often new halls are built with no planned storage space for playgroups, even though the hall is being built to replace an old one which was already housing a playgroup.

RESTRICTIONS

There is real fear that under-fives may damage property. This is regrettable but understandable in a generation which often finds grandchildren unbearably noisy, and deduces from the wreckage of cheap, shoddy toys that they are destructive also —and many grandparents sit on the committees which form hall policies. It is less easy to understand how people can refuse under-fives the use of youth clubs, on the grounds that they will 'spoil it for the older ones'. Naturally enough, sand and water are banned from many of the beautiful floors intended for dancing. But could the floor not be covered by a drugget? And need the kitchen sink also be out of bounds for water play?

It is a pleasure to be able to record the warm hospitality offered by many hall committees. Cupboards and shelves are built; rails are put up in corridors on which the works of art are pinned and left to delight subsequent hall-users; and often extra rooms are made available at no extra charge. Many caretakers, too, enter into the spirit of the venture; they mend toys, put out the equipment in the morning, help to clear it away, come in to watch the children—and even put in an early word at jumble sales if they see something they feel would be useful to the playgroup.

In theory, no one would deny that a new, attractive, purpose-built hall would be ideal—but experience tends to show that an old and rather dingy hall may be even more rewarding. Such halls have inspired group decorating sessions, and even plumbing and wiring has been undertaken by willing fathers. One small hall could not be put into use until the fathers had dug over 100 yards of trench in order to lay on water, while the mothers decorated and made curtains—no wonder this group radiated such joy and purpose. Better an old hall used freely and creatively than a beautiful new one that inhibits the children. But would it not be possible to plan new premises with playgroups in mind? Could there not be a purpose-built store room, with a window, washable floor, sink and tap? When all the equipment had been put in the hall, this small room would be available for sand and water play.

OUTDOOR PLAYSPACE

This is highly desirable, especially in areas where children may have no other opportunity of having contact with living and growing things. They need to be out of doors, to be introduced to the wind, clouds, frost, ice, snow, mud and dust; they need to dig, examine worms and insects; plant seeds; pick growing flowers (one nasturtium seed in a large pot will provide a long succession of flowers).

Sometimes outdoor space needs to be cleared, or fenced. Often local planning permission is given for the erection of a specified type of wall or fence, providing the playgroup pays for it—the cost has been known to be as high as £400. Sometimes the labour involved in removing dilapidated outhouses, and the accumulated rubbish of years, is too great for people already stretched to their limit.

PLAYGROUP LEADERS

It does not always follow that, because a playgroup leader is an NNEB, SRN, Infant or Junior teacher, or the holder of a degree, she is automatically better at working with three- and four-year-olds and their mothers than someone untrained. Some good playgroups are run by mothers, or others, who had no training for anything after leaving school, or who had an apparently irrelevant training. However, it is already clear that *whether or not* playgroup leaders were previously qualified, they would be helped by a specially designed Playgroup Course.

Perhaps this was one of the most difficult lessons I had to learn; it is enlightening to see someone untrained running a first-class playgroup. Possibly we forget how much learning and growing can go on throughout our lives. What one *is* matters in this field of human relationships even more that what one *knows*. For this reason it is worth repeating clearly:

1. 'Relevant trainings' are no guarantee for making good playgroup leaders.

2. Untrained mothers, and others, can do excellent work.

The value of specially planned playgroup courses is already clear. Even good teachers have acknowledged the help that they needed before undertaking the extra dimension of mother-involvement in playgroup work.

RECOMMENDATIONS TO THOSE ABOUT TO BE REGISTERED

1. Please avoid the term Nursery School or Play School when seeking for a name for your new group.

2. Make contact with the local voluntary area organizer or the local branch of PPA—they will see to it that you have all the help and advice that they can give you from their own experience.

3. Be sure that you, and your playgroup, are adequately insured. PPA offers a special Playgroup Insurance Policy, but the suggestion still needs to be made at the time of registering in case a group fails to make contact with PPA.

4. Visit as many nursery schools and playgroups as you can before starting your own.

5. Attend a playgroup course if there is one available.

RECOMMENDATIONS TO SOCIAL SERVICES DEPARTMENTS

1. That registration shall fall into two parts:

   (*a*) The registration of premises.

(*b*) The permission to start the playgroup, which should be withheld until the people concerned and the equipment provided reach reasonable levels of readiness.

2. That no playgroup shall be registered for more than twenty-four children, however big the hall may be. (The extra four will allow for absence, and make all the difference to the finances.)
The reasons for this recommendation are:

(*a*) Twenty children, one or two mothers, and a helper constitute the maximum number to whom even a good playgroup leader can give her full attention.
(*b*) The overall weakness of playgroups is that the level of noise is too high. The presence of nineteen other children is more than enough for the twentieth.

3. That hall rents are negotiated, when necessary, on behalf of those who want to start a playgroup. In so many cases, those who most need a low rent are unable to meet the committee concerned to put their case adequately, still less are they able to exert any pressure.

4. That persuasion should be brought to bear on hall committees refusing to allow storage cupboards to be installed because it would spoil the appearance of the premises. Too many playgroup people accept this and continue to work under quite unreasonable conditions.

Chapter 8

Various aspects of cost

These vary greatly. Many churches allow playgroups to use their halls rent free, but the playgroups give a donation to cover the cost of heating and caretaking. Some halls charge £5 for a three-hour session. Some halls charge £1 per hour; sometimes a system of heating has been installed that was appropriate for its intended use, but the playgroup finds that it costs £1 an hour for heat alone. Some halls charge a high rent, and then use the residual heat in the room for their own afternoon functions. Some halls charge a nominal rent, say 40p, and the vicar goes in daily at 6.30 a.m. to light the aged stove in order that the room shall be warm by 9 a.m. Others charge a low rent in return for the mothers becoming regular caretakers.

Some Education Committees allow disused schools, youth club premises or adult education centres to be used rent free, the cost of heating to be met by the playgroup. Playgroups are run in village halls, church halls, Women's Institute halls, community centres, scout huts, sports pavilions, political party halls and others besides. Each hall committee fixes its own rent, usually in accordance with what it imagines to be the financial state of the playgroup. Two factors are often overlooked: if the children are to play as frequently as they need, the cost must be kept low. Rents need to vary between the peppercorn and £2 per session if playgroups are to function realistically; and play-groups have hidden costs. The playgroup is sometimes to blame when rents are unrealistic for they have failed to explain their expenses over and above the rent and the payment for the leader.

On the other hand, some committees see the regular letting of their hall to the playgroup as a means of making money; this is particularly difficult to justify in those cases where the hall is already heated during the morning, whether or not it is in use. Is it not better to receive a small rent than none at all? Do committee members realize just how much effort lies behind the payment of this rent? Much more careful communication is needed between hall and playgroup committees if neither is to feel 'used' by the other.

DEPRECIATION FOR HOUSE PLAYGROUPS

Mention of this should be made. People tend to assume that because a playgroup pays no rent in a house, then a large profit is being made.

Many wives do pay their husbands' 'rent', and careful book-keeping is available for income tax purposes.

Even when a formal payment is not made, the fact remains that extra rooms are heated, timber is bought for the construction of shelves and cupboards, walls are more frequently redecorated and carpets receive extra wear.

In many cases large sums of money have already been spent on installing extra toilets and washbasins, rendering doors and ceilings fireproof, and frequently building an extension especially for the playgroup.

PLAYGROUP LEADERS' PAYMENTS

Many playgroup leaders work for no payment for a year or more, until the playgroup is safely established and the children have adequate equipment. The average payment seems to be between £1 and £1·50 for a three-hour session for the playgroup leader, and 75p and £1 for her regular helpers. These people are literally working for love and this token payment is seen as such.

Some churches will only allow a playgroup to use their hall if all the help is voluntary. This can have unfortunate repercussions, for there tends to be a succession of playgroup leaders, and the children never know whom to expect. It should be remembered that giving up three or four mornings a week can be expensive on the housekeeping, for mid-day dinners have to be prepared quickly, once the playgroup is over, with expensive frozen foods which are quicker than hand-prepared vegetables —costs soon mount.

But another important issue arises: should the mothers of the children *want* to take advantage of permanent voluntary labour, especially if this help is given several times a week? It should be remembered that a three-hour play session usually means four hours work, for it takes half an hour to set up and clear away the activities (more if the storage is particularly inadequate).

One of the chief joys of playgroup leaders who earn a little money is being able to buy their husbands' birthday and Christmas presents with money that has not been saved from the housekeeping—this has been the most frequent comment of all when they have spoken of their earnings.

The difference between a salary and a token payment is important. An adequate salary might tempt some people to stay on indefinitely, growing stale or else dominating the mothers by their competence. Worse still, some people might apply for such posts because it seemed a congenial and convenient way of earning good money, and some groups of mothers lack the confidence to sack a wrong choice.

Many playgroup leaders work for a token payment for several years, and then the need for more money (or a professional training) leads them to move on, leaving the way clear for someone else to grow in stature and take her place. Such leaders, knowing that they are not intending to stay indefinitely, take pride and joy in delegating responsibility to parents—whose response and growth delights them as much as the children.

HIDDEN COSTS

1. *Insurance and/or Industrial Injury stamps.*

2. *Playgroup insurance.*[1]

The necessity of adequate insurance cannot be over-emphasized. Some groups are not insured for anything, not even for third party claims related to the children in their care. (Should it not be a legal obligation? Recent court awards suggest that a minimum cover of £100,000 would be well advised.) Every

[1] PPA has its own scheme for members: £5 per annum for a basic comprehensive cover, or £7 to include personal accident liability.

employee should be covered for employers' liability, and technically a certificate to this effect should be exhibited at the place of employment.

3. *The morning snack.* Fruit juice, biscuits, apples, carrots, etc. are provided at no extra cost to the children. Free milk can be obtained, but since the ministry repays three months in arrears some groups feel unable to cope with the records and the money.

4. *Toilet requisites; paper towels and tissues.* Some groups have no facilities for hanging towels on pegs, and if children bring their own towels each day there is the complication of seeing that each one is put into its owner's carrier bag or satchel.

Toilet rolls. Some halls lock up their supply, and if the playgroups leave their own toilet rolls on the premises then these have gone the following day. So not only do they have to be provided, but locked up with the equipment at the end of each session.

Soap. Most groups seem to provide their own, also their washing-up liquid.

5. *Expendable equipment.* Flour and salt (for dough); powder paint; glue of various types for various purposes; paper; sellotape; first aid items (often including the regular purchase of disinfectant for the toilets); and stationery for notes, invitations, notices of jumble sales, etc.

COST TO PARENTS

This is based on the out-going expenses referred to above. Because it is the rent which varies more than any other factor, the charges to the children vary quite widely. Twenty-four per cent of playgroups charge 20p or less per session; 51 per cent charge between 21p and 30p; 25 per cent charge over 30p.

The attendance of children at playgroups is not always dependent upon the family income: spending priorities are highly personal, and relevant. The following examples show some of the variations in the pattern of payment.

1. A council estate in a particular area may house a majority

of families who are deprived in many respects, including financially. It may be essential to keep the cost down to 5p or 8p, and some committees allow their hearts to overrule their heads to the extent of not making a charge if the children are absent. This may mean that the first wet or foggy day reduces the number of children from twenty to five. Or an epidemic of measles can have the same effect, but for a longer period. In these circumstances, not only does the playgroup leader find herself without payment, but the rent has to be covered from the Committee's private purses.

Mothers in these areas would find it hard, both financially and emotionally, to 'pay for what they haven't had', so payment in arrears is out. And so, almost always, is monthly payment in advance. The happiest solution seems to be for mothers to pay two weeks in advance at the beginning of a term, and once a week thereafter. In this way there is always a week's money in hand to offset against illness; and mothers are less likely to keep children away for casual days if they know they have already paid for them.

2. In some apparently poor areas, mothers have been known to offer 'double pay if you'll let me off rota duty', some add that they pay 25p an hour for baby-sitters when they go out with their husbands, 'so 50p a morning's still dirt cheap'.

3. In some areas the mothers find life so difficult that they are only able to get through each day if they are buoyed up by the thought of a personal pleasure in the evening. One such mother stopped her daughter's attendance at the playgroup (two mornings at 13p each) because she 'couldn't afford it', and to substantiate her claim she volunteered a budget statement ending with £1·75 for Bingo. The playgroup leader suggested a compromise whereby the mother had £1·50 for Bingo while the child had three sessions for 25p. The reply was, 'Christ! You must have *something* for yourself!' This cry must be taken seriously; until the children are easier to manage, and the mother makes friendships that are rewarding, she will continue to need this nightly escape.

4. In some areas mothers have said, 'Let's all pay an extra 2½p a day so there's a fund to cover needy children.'

5. In some areas mothers who cannot pay in cash pay in kind—they *ask* to clean the room each day, or look after the dressing-up clothes and wash them each week.

6. In some areas where mothers say they cannot afford 20p a session, the children play at home alone in expensive pedal cars, or with fabulous dolls' prams. It takes time for such attitudes to change, and it can only come about by word of mouth, as playgroup mothers enthuse about this new experience in their lives.

7. In at least one area, prone to strikes and short pay packets, the playgroup leader instituted a plan whereby each mother brought her weekly money in a specially provided two inch square envelope. It was an unwritten law that everyone handed in her envelope each week, even if it was empty. This saved face and they were all left free to make up the money later if they could, or to forget it with a clear conscience if they could not. Up to the time of speaking to me about it, the playgroup leader said that no one had ever taken advantage of this situation, and those who had been unable to make up all the money had helped in countless practical ways; or even raised the money by making a cake and raffling it among the other mothers.

8. Sometimes parents pay by cheque, a term in advance; sometimes they pay in cash, a term in advance for two of their children.

9. Some playgroups ask for £1 deposit when the child first joins, to be refunded when he leaves. In the early days of a playgroup this helps to provide equipment quickly. Other groups charge 25p registration fee. It is interesting to note that in some very deprived areas this is accepted without question, and not once has this been reclaimed if the child failed to accept the vacancy when it was offered.

10. In some areas the income from the children never covers the outgoing expenses, and fund-raising is a permanent part of the playgroup scene. Jumble sales are probably the greatest stand-by, but often the jumble has to be provided from other sources since those who thankfully wear jumble are not in a

position to provide it. In these areas bring-and-buy stalls and small raffles are welcomed, as long as tickets are cheap—four 2p tickets offer a better chance than two 4p tickets; and if there is only 2p to spare, then it's still a chance worth taking and no harm done.

Part III

The Birth and Development of the Pre-school Playgroups Association (PPA)

Chapter 9

The Pre-school Playgroups Association

Parents had a difficult time during the war years—the choice to evacuate the children or not was a new dilemma in our society. The children who were evacuated suffered the shock of separation and later the second shock of being uprooted yet again to go back to a mother who was sometimes less real to them than their foster parents. Fathers came back to be greeted by strangers; and when the children had been born while the fathers were abroad there was often an emotional blank that was never adequately filled. It was the children who were three and four years old at the outbreak of war who had to grow through this turbulent period before becoming parents of three- and four-year-olds in 1960.

At this time Belle Tutaev brought into being her first playgroup, started for the sake of her own child, and she wrote a letter to the *Guardian*, saying that she would gladly offer help and advice to anyone wanting to do the same thing. There was a flood of replies from all over the country.

From this one letter the playgroup movement snowballed; from one child in 1961 to approximately 360,000 in 1976. The time was right, not only for the limelight to focus on the under-fives, but also on the needs of their parents. It was only later that the parents began to realize just how much they were benefiting themselves, and the principle of parent involvement was born.

Even though membership more or less doubled each year for the next three or four years, the numbers remained small enough for the family feeling to predominate. And as new

107

playgroups were encouraged by personal contact, the idea of parent involvement was perpetuated by example and personal explanation.

Then the idea began to spread. Motives for starting playgroups were by no means always altruistic, and parent involvement did not appeal to many of the newcomers, but the concept of parent involvement as an integral part of the playgroup was staunchly adhered to by the pioneers who started playgroups.

VOLUNTARY ORGANIZERS

Area

As founder members took it upon themselves to offer help to new playgroups starting in their own areas, what was more natural than their becoming known as voluntary area organizers?

Originally it was a question of befriending, advising, visiting; making personal contact with the Medical Officer of Health to offer help to those about to start playgroups; making contact with the education authorities to ask for grants (almost never available); or for help with courses for those realizing that they did not know enough.

In those early days it was exhausting and often thankless work. The idea was too new; there was no money in local authority coffers; the under-fives were 'nothing to do with education'.[1] Over-burdened Health Authorities had their work cut out to inspect and pass premises and intending playgroup leaders, and many were reluctant to involve themselves additionally in being concerned about the quality of play.

Now, nearly thirteen years later, there are new lessons to be learned, and the first residential weekends for area organizers have been held both north and south of the border, as they try to build the future on the past. In a sense pre-school education is accepted as a necessity, and playgroups have become part of our national way of life; PPA is an acknowledged influence in their development, and in the evolution of playgroup courses for those involved in the work.

There is less need for pacemakers, and more for peace-

---

[1] A PPA publication, 'Local Authorities and Playgroups', lists the precise clauses in the various acts under which help *can* be given.

makers; the birth pangs are over and development is calling for new qualities. An area organizer needs to have an awareness of her own strengths and weaknesses, to be able to pace herself, and to be able to recognize different temperaments and person-alities, in order that she shall not expect too much, or too little, from those with whom she works.

Everyone has many strengths, and several weaknesses. The weaknesses may not matter—as long as they are known. In many counties there is a splendid team built up on the strength of knowing weaknesses. It's a case of 'I'm hopeless visiting playgroups, but I'm good on organization'; or 'I love the mothers and children, but I get letters and money into a ghastly muddle.'

An ambassador to local authorities and councillors needs to be someone who inspires confidence; someone who can marshal her facts; who knows what to ask for, and when to ask for it; who knows the code of professional etiquette with reference to letters, telephone calls, interviews.

The personality of area organizers visiting playgroups is all-important. Some, with the best will in the world, leave a play-group ruffled, unsure, or even downright angry. Others revive morale, inspire, and are instrumental in helping a poor play-group to become a valuable one. Others have no effect at all, the playgroup people are quite pleased to see her, quite enjoy her visit, and are quite glad to see her go. Considerable maturity is needed if visiting is to achieve tangible results.

Speaking engagements come thick and fast, to speak to Women's Institutes, Young Wives, Townswomen's Guilds, Parent-Teacher Associations, the local councillors or a new playgroup. Area organizers who do this need to be free of bees in their bonnets. Dogmatism is likely to defeat the very points they most wish to make. Help is needed by most area organizers before they feel ready to speak to open meetings.

Area organizers need to know where to send people with special needs; each of them needs a list of local names and addresses of associations, clinics, departments, and to know the channels through which they can be approached.

There are now over three hundred area organizers, and among them are many outstanding women. Sadly, many people are prevented from doing this work for lack of finance. Travelling expenses need to be realistic, and hidden expenses recognized—it is not always possible to do baby-sitting on a reciprocal basis.

Broadly speaking, area organizers fall into two categories, the short term and the long term.

Short-term area organizers. These are likely to be women involved in the running of their own playgroups, whose interest and abilities have grown to the point when they feel able to respond to the needs of other playgroup people. Powers of leadership and organization grow as people turn to them and lean on them: their concern overrides their diffidence, and they undertake the daunting task of establishing contact with the various local authorities in order to ask for local playgroup courses, facilities for bulk buying through the educational supplies officer, grants from local charities for playgroups with special needs, rent reductions, transport for needy children, speakers for meetings, etc. Sometimes they are stretched, strained and 'used' to near breaking point, and in their turn they need someone to lean on. The more experienced area organizers and the members of the national executive committee offer personal support by letter, phone and visits during these periods of stress, but in many cases this personal support and encouragement comes from the very members of the local authority who had once seemed so awe-inspiring and distant.

The most characteristic comment of these new area organizers is 'If anyone had told me a year ago that I should be doing these things, I would never have believed them!'

After two or three years their own children have gone on to school, and the sphere of interest changes; or lack of money sends them into part-time employment; or husbands feel that the situation is growing out-of-hand, and call for readjustment. Whatever the reason, they resign from their voluntary appointment, and both they and PPA are equally grateful to the other.

Long-term area organizers. Quite often these are older women who have been in the playgroup movement from the beginning, but some who thought they would only be 'short

FOOTNOTE 1976
In 1971 the DES gave an additional grant for a second National Adviser and the Scottish PPA received a grant for their first National Adviser. In 1972 a DHSS grant enabled the appointment of six Training and Development Officers.

term' find that they wish to continue. They have learned to balance home commitments; their knowledge of playgroups is comprehensive; they have a grasp of the local situation, and the wisdom and ability to handle emotional crises; they have established good relationships with the local authorities and are adept at encouraging new playgroups in the areas that most need them.

Many of these women are driven by a quiet conviction that what they are doing is worthwhile and several of them have undertaken part-time employment in another sphere in order to earn enough money to continue their voluntary work without detriment to the family. But now many of these women are resigning, and the playgroup movement can ill afford to lose some of them. There are three main reasons for their resignation.

Firstly, many have gone on to do teacher training, in the certainty that they want to work professionally with children and parents for the next twenty years. Secondly, the strain of both a money-earning job and the work of an area organizer is too great. And the one cannot be continued without the other. And thirdly, those who have worked gladly and voluntarily for many years eventually reach the point where they feel that they must make a financial contribution to the family; so they resign, and all too frequently become squarish-pegs in money-earning round holes.

Sometimes these women apply for local posts as playgroup advisers. But sometimes they have no paper qualifications, or their previous training was (apparently) irrelevant, and they feel unable to apply. Yet their worth in the playgroup field is proven. What is the answer?

One answer is for a local authority grant to be given to the branch or county association, to be spent in the way that would most benefit the non-profit-making playgroups. In this sort of situation the committee usually decides that nothing is as valuable as someone to give advice and support, so the 'right person' is sought.

There may be no obvious adviser, but a very obvious tower of strength and wisdom in the person of the unqualified, or irrelevantly qualified, area organizer. In such a situation, there may be a unanimous decision to appoint her to do exactly what she is at present doing voluntarily: from then on everyone has

111

a clear conscience, and the relationship between the members, their newly acquired status symbol, and the local authorities becomes clean cut, professional and more effective. But such a person usually prefers to be called an organizer rather than an adviser.

In one county such an organizer was appointed for a year by the County Association of PPA when a local trust fund gave a once-only gift of £100. The energy and purpose that followed from this honorarium were out of all proportion to the gift. At the end of the year the honorarium became a salary, subsidised by a grant from the Local Education Authority. Later, the (then) Health Department and Education Department jointly paid the salary and expenses of a part-time advisory teacher, who was appointed to complement the work of the organizer. The work is shared, each having knowledge and experience that overlaps the other's, but each finding that she is making her own niche in the playgroup community.

The organizer finds that queries directed to her tend to fall into four categories:

People.   How do you cope with apathetic parents?
How do you manage a rota, or other voluntary help?
How do you decide who is paid, and who is not?
What do other people pay staff? How do you pay them?
Who needs National Insurance, Industrial Injuries Insurance?
Where are the courses? Who can attend? Can people be sponsored to attend by, say, the playgroup committee?

Premises.   Rent, heating and other costs—what do others pay?
Why do some church halls charge no rent but ask for a donation instead?
How do you use storage to the best advantage?
Do you need written agreements about rent and the use of the hall?
How do you learn to get on with hall committees and other landlords and caretakers?
What sort of insurance do you need for children, staff and equipment? What is covered by the landlord?

Administration. How do you form a committee and adopt a constitution?

How do you inform parents about costs and other money matters?

How do you explain when fees have to be increased to meet rising costs?

How do you charge? Hourly? Daily? Weekly? Term in advance?

Do you charge when children are away?

What do you do if you don't get the payment?

What do other people charge?

How do you hold a parents' meeting to sort out money or staff problems?

Open days and publicity.   How do you overcome local hostility or lack of interest?

What are the legal requirements about raising money?

How do you link up with the local primary school?

How do you get to see other playgroups?

How can you get them to see that you don't want to criticize, but you want to see what they do?

How do you involve secondary school girls? Boys too?

This organizer adds 'Sometimes I feel that the most I can be is a listening ear, and someone able to suggest solutions, or where they could find the help, advice or information that they require.' Her own acquired knowledge on these matters is now considerable, and although much of it can be disseminated during playgroup courses there comes a time in the life of most playgroups when they need someone to sit down with them all to discuss the burning issue of the moment.

Playgroups are penetrating ever more deeply into areas where the above questions are too difficult to be solved without outside help; and if the adviser has to attend to this side of the work, what will become of the endless queue waiting for advice on how to cope with difficult children, and how to arrange a room to the best advantage, all of which are additional to her tutoring playgroup courses? Both aspects of the work need to be covered. This needs to be stressed, for already valuable area organizers are saying, 'Now an adviser is appointed there's obviously no need for me.'

A good playgroup is an extension of the home for both mother and child (father too, whenever possible) and the social servicing

is just as important as the educational servicing. Both are essential.

The Scottish Social Work Services Group sponsored a series of residential conferences, with expenses paid, for playgroup organizers. Those invited to the conference included representatives of local authorities, the voluntary area organizers of the Scottish PPA, and representatives of the Church of Scotland. If playgroups are to be relevant to their own communities there must be time for those working in widely different areas to meet, talk, think and plan together. This is especially true when it comes to working at training courses at various levels.

One residential weekend deserves special mention. It was arranged as a family occasion, and accommodation was booked in a chalet hotel: for some it was the first time they had stayed in a hotel as a family, and the children were filled with a sense of occasion. During the daytime fathers took children swimming, riding, exploring or to the zoo. But it was during the Saturday evening that the most valuable period came, when the husbands began to talk about their own attitudes to their wives' involvement with playgroups. Several wives commented that they had never heard their husbands so articulate before; neither had they realized that their husbands were proud of them, and that the usual banter hid real pleasure.

County

Many counties now have more than half a dozen area organizers, and in order to streamline organization, and cut down on unnecessary travelling in such a situation they often appoint one of their number to be the county organizer. Local authorities find it less confusing to deal with one person, and in addition to forming the link between the local authorities and the playgroup people she is also to co-ordinate the work of the team of area organizers. Whether or not she still has time for visiting playgroups depends on geography in many areas, though most feel

FOOTNOTE 1976
In 1973 the Welsh Office gave a grant for the first National Adviser for Wales and the DHSS grant was increased for two more Training and Development Officers. In 1974 the DES increased its grant for a third National Adviser and the DHSS grant was increased again. In 1975 the Welsh Office grant was increased to appoint three part-time Development Officers. In 1976 the DHSS increased its grant again.

114

the need to keep in close touch with the children in their local setting.

BRANCHES

The one thing above all others that playgroup people need is to be able to exchange ideas, compare notes, and seek solutions to common problems. So branches came into being, starting with two or more playgroups which were members of PPA, having a constitution that was acceptable to the Department of Education and Science as being of charitable status, and officers who were individual members of PPA. This closed shop lasted for some time, for members still felt at this point that only by banding together to proclaim the value of parent involvement could they hope to make any local, or national impact.

It was possible to stipulate that playgroups had to have at least one member who belonged to PPA though it was not possible to guarantee that all the playgroups were a good advertisement for PPA. It was possible to stipulate that play-groups had to have parent involvement, but precisely what constituted involvement? Some mothers did their rota duty, but felt press-ganged rather than involved; others did not do rota duty but felt themselves to be deeply involved with each other and the playgroup. The standards and styles of the playgroups varied widely. Who was competent to decide, and how, which were good playgroups? And what could be done about bad groups?

In 1967 membership began to rise steeply, but non-PPA playgroups began to proliferate even more rapidly, and quantity prevailed over quality. Concern for children in these playgroups outside the branch moved several branches to reconsider the PPA-playgroup-only rule: many of them came to the independent conclusion that children mattered more than rules, and they threw membership open to everyone. It worked, up to a point, for at least isolates were drawn together in a branch; they were invited to visit other playgroups; they had a chance to consider other ways of running groups; they had a chance to hear informed speakers and to see films and exhibitions of children's genuine unaided painting and makings. The National Executive recognized the wisdom in this new thinking, and the ruling was changed; only the branch officers were required to be PPA members. This was considered to be essential lest the branch itself lost the inspiration towards which the enlightened members worked.

In some areas the Directors of Education furthered PPA's aims by only giving the concession of buying materials and equipment cheaply through the supplies officer to branch members: this brought in even more members. The fact that they joined for reasons of personal gain was considered immaterial— what mattered was that there was now a chance to influence the playgroups indirectly for the benefit of the children.

The branches and area organizers became the strongest force for good in the playgroup world, together with the proliferation of playgroup courses, and precious time spared by a few local authority advisers and playgroup course tutors. Often the branches had grown directly out of the first course to be held in an area, for at the end of it people wanted to go on meeting together.

Some of the present 300 branches are so highly organized, and have proved to be so effective, that local authorities are making them grants. The amounts can vary from £25 to £9000 (1971) and the purpose may be specified or unspecified.[1]

COUNTY ASSOCIATIONS

It is largely a question of geography that decides whether the first coming-together of playgroups shall be to form a branch or a county association.

It is almost always young urban families moving out to rural areas who start playgroups in the country; their own needs are as urgent as those of their children, and they will travel miles to make contact with someone else running a playgroup. Eventually the few pioneers decide to band together officially in order to be able to negotiate more effectively with local authorities. Many of them realize that strangers of a few years' residence in a village are unlikely to be listened to, so they ask local people in public life if they would set the wheels in motion. This works well, and a county association is launched with strong local backing.

When such a county association calls a committee meeting in

---

1 By 1976 the total of local authority grants was £500,000 of which £300,000 was contributed by Education and Social Services departments in the Inner London area.

the first year or two of its existence it is not at all unusual for members to travel 150 miles (at their own cost) to attend. But slowly the movement gathers momentum, and eventually branches begin to spring up, usually in the areas where the first enthusiasts live.

In some areas the first branch draws members together from isolated areas all over the county. Usually they carry the whole burden themselves, and struggle on without outside help until membership widens enough for the first unwieldy branch to split up into smaller branches. In other areas local branches come first, and are later co-ordinated by a county association.

REGIONS

The first regions, formed in 1967, were the Scottish and Irish Pre-school Playgroups Associations. Each has its own executive committee and constitution, and works within a framework related to local laws; but both these regions feel themselves to be integral parts of the whole Pre-school Playgroups Association.

The third region to be formed was the south west. This was a natural geographical development for here isolation is more than a matter of miles. Cornwall has so much coastline that there is only one direction in which to travel for help. There was only a single playgroup in Cornwall to begin with, and the pioneers were drawn towards Bristol and Devonshire for support. So it came about that Exeter became the focal point for trains and cars, and a region slowly came into being. Growing enthusiasm for playgroups later led to the formation of the Cornish Association for the Pre-School Child, and the Devonshire Pre-School Playgroups Association. Now branches are forming within the county associations.

Flexibility has been the keyword at every stage, for situations have to be accepted as they are, rather than as an administrator would wish them to be.[1]

WHAT OF THE FUTURE?

The principle of live and let live has worked well; on the whole,

[1] There are now (1976) independent associations in Scotland and Northern Ireland and ten regions in England, with Wales as the newly established eleventh region. Nine of the regions have regional offices.

the low-populated areas started with large regional or county associations, and are breaking down into branch units. The more populated areas started with branches, and are working up and outward to form county associations and regions.

The aim is to form regions to coincide with Her Majesty's Inspectorate divisions, these to come naturally and in their own good time. In this sort of organization you do not say to over-worked young parents, 'You've got to link with your three neighbouring counties before next year; get cracking!' As and when it happens (and it is coming) each region will elect its representative to the national executive Committee.

MEMBERSHIP

This is currently (1973) under review, for live and let live is easy enough when 'the others' are 'over there'. Now the country is being welded into a whole, the much more difficult give-and-take phase has arrived. The struggle to provide an ever-growing income, whilst trying to mount an even faster growing daily service, will continue. Those who need most time and attention can least afford to contribute towards the cost of its provision. The national association is working towards a form of subscription that will incorporate both local and national membership and be acceptable to a diversity of playgroups.

THE NATIONAL EXECUTIVE COMMITTEE

The national executive committee is composed of members nominated by the regions, plus such co-options as are needed, and ex-officio members. All of them come from within the movement itself. To confine a committee with such heavy responsibilities to young unknowns might seem to some to be irresponsible, yet this apparent weakness is probably PPA'S greatest strength.

Throughout nine years of working with this slowly changing committee (members are appointed for three years, with re-election giving a maximum of six years) it has become apparent that again and again the professional answer would have been the wrong answer. It is precisely because these men and women know the job that they are so willing and able to seek new ways of meeting new needs. It is because almost all of them are parents, professionals in their own sphere, do-it-yourself decorators, children's sick-room attendants, cooks, householders, neighbours, marriage partners and voluntary workers, that they know from present personal experience the strains placed upon modern families. It is because they constantly needed to be listened to, understood and guided by nursery school and other professionals in their early playgroup days that they come to the national executive committee so ready both to go on listening to the members and to continue to seek guidance themselves.

The first break away from promotion from the ranks came when Dr W. D. Wall, Dean of the Institute of Education in London University, became a very active President, constantly available for discussion and advice at a very critical period. Personal consultation is also continuous with the Department of Health and Social Security, the Home Office, the Social Work Services Group in Scotland, and the Department of Education and Science. Contact with the latter has been particularly close in view of the fact that it was their grant to PPA in 1967 which made a three-year survey of playgroups possible:[1] each new stage of development concerning playgroup courses has been put before them, the failures as well as the successes, as careful progress is made towards a nationally recognized series of playgroup courses; and a cautious start was made on the first experimental tutors' course in 1969.

During the time of writing the professions represented on the committee have included a doctor and vicar, several graduates, several teachers, two Froebel nursery school teachers, a Froebel training college lecturer, a graduate chartered accountant, a company secretary, a biologist, a personnel officer, two child care officers, a statistician and researcher, a journalist and editor, two secretaries, a nurse, and two ministers' wives. Several of them had worked in deeply deprived areas, and almost without exception they had worked in playgroups. But the unbroken chain of experience runs through the movement, from the mothers and children in the playgroups up through

[1] This grant has been renewed annually since 1970; in 1971 it was doubled and a second National Adviser was appointed by PPA. In 1973 the Welsh Office made a grant for another National Adviser, and in 1974 the DES grant was doubled again.

119

the playgroup leaders, the area organizers, the county organizers and the regional representatives to the executive.

The consolidated experience of the last fifteen years has crystallized into the recognition that the emphasis has widened from 'What can we do to help children?' to 'What can we do to help parents to help their own children, thereby becoming happier people themselves?' This new situation calls for new thinking, and the combined experience of each successive committee is highly relevant to the task in hand.

THE CENTRAL OFFICE

This has progressed slowly from papers kept in chests of drawers, boxes and suitcases in members' homes to more official quarters in 1966. This first office was two rooms in a condemned tenement, decorated by members who left a second-hand portable typewriter and a gay geranium in a pot to welcome the first part-time helper who rejoiced in the dignified title 'Office Staff'. Before sitting down to work she went to buy an old desk, a single chair and two trestle tables. Work multiplied alarmingly, and another part-time helper was appointed for whom another desk and chair were found: membership was now 1500, and a well-used duplicator and some gas heaters were purchased.

In 1968 the demolition date arrived, and two tiny rooms were rented in Southwark. By this time the membership was 7500 and additional help was needed at crisis points: there were by then two new typewriters, an electric duplicating machine, an addressograph and, eventually, a plate-making machine with various attachments.

Two years later a basement room was rented for the storage and packing of publications, but even this proved to be inadequate for the 10,000 booklets and pamphlets sent out each year. The gallery of a chapel in Leighton Buzzard was used to store the overflow, and when an additional 40,000 copies of *Playgroup News* arrived each term one member's family car had to stand in the garden while the bundles of *Playgroup News* took up the cubic space which it formerly occupied.

Additional part-time help for the original stalwarts was provided, and a telephone installed for outgoing calls (incoming ones would have disrupted the work disastrously).

Between eighty and a hundred letters were being answered each day, in addition to the renewal of thousands of subscriptions, the duplicating of executive papers, Branch and Area Organizers' newsletters, and reports from the NEC officers and national adviser.

The pressure mounted as space dwindled, and life became so difficult that mercifully it became a joke.

In 1969 a grant from the National Playing Fields Association enabled the PPA to appoint a part-time General Secretary: the first holder of this post had been one of the founder members of PPA, and had served six years on the national executive committee. Her appointment enabled her to leave her teaching post, and to spend time transferring a prodigious amount of information from her head into a comprehensive filing system. It also enabled committees to meet having been fully briefed by comprehensive sets of papers previously circulated. It would be difficult to overestimate the value of this servicing, also of the personal links that were forged with individuals at national level.

This grant was renewed annually until 1975 and the debt of gratitude PPA owes the NPFA for its timely help is incalculable.

DEVELOPMENTS

1. *Contact* (the Association's magazine)
This began as a personal, duplicated newsletter written by Belle Tutaev as she diligently kept the first enthusiasts in touch with each other. It grew to be a small printed magazine, and established the principle of keeping people in contact with each other (hence its name), and of sharing news and views.

By 1975 it had changed to an A4 format, still issued ten times a year, with a constant thirty-two pages and a circulation around 15,000.

Contact's primary aim is to keep playgroup supervisors in touch as they learn from children, parents, courses and each other. But it also links those whose interest has widened to include teenagers and children with special needs in playgroups, Mother and Toddler Clubs, a wide field of commitment within the Association, and a lively interest in wider topics.

As the playgroup movement spread, new needs arose that

Contact could not meet without modifications that would not appeal to its enthusiastic readers. Instead of trying to be all things to all people it was decided to launch a separate publication.

2. *Under-5*
This periodical was launched in 1975 and is produced four times a year, also in A4 format, with a circulation of around 100,000.

The aim is to fill the gap between women's magazines and those centred on bringing up children or homemaking. It is not aimed solely at playgroup parents, but it is based on the playgroup ethos that parents learn best from each other. It assumes that parents love their children; that being a parent is enough to try the patience of a saint at times; that money isn't plentiful; that handy-men and women aren't all that handy; that parents are thoughtful even when they aren't 'clever'; and that the laughter of shared experience is a tonic.[1]

3. *Publications*
These have all been written at the request of the Publications Committee, and the people who have tried to meet the demands made on them have all done so without payment of any kind.

The first needs were for 'Starting a Playgroup', and a 'Supervisor's Handbook'. These have been revised in the light of widening experience, and other needs have been met by nearly thirty different publications.

The aim is to reach the maximum number of people as cheaply as possible while keeping a standard that commands respect, and in a form that is so practical and direct that it can be understood by playgroup people everywhere. In the same way that *Contact* needed its counterpart in *Playgroup News*, so some of these publications now need their simpler counterparts. Recognition of this fact is an indication of how surely the playgroup movement is penetrating those areas where it is most needed.

It is important to stress that every single publication is written from first-hand experience: it is felt that at this stage only those

---

[1] *Playgroup News* preceded *Under-5*, and its four pioneering years taught us that the mothers wanted something less playgroup-oriented and more appealing to the eye.

who have done should write. It would be easier to put the writing on to less burdened shoulders, but authenticity of experience is the key to the growth of the movement.

4. *Television and Radio*

Bristol's BBC Further Education Television producer Eileen Molony has championed the cause of playgroups and it is to be hoped that this will be developed even further. The first series was three programmes on 'How to Start a Playgroup'; this was followed up in the autumn of 1970 by a series of five programmes on 'Improving your Playgroup' and these were repeated three months later.

Then came Tyne Tees *Play with a Purpose* in twenty-six weekly instalments, updated and re-shot in colour four years later.

In co-operation with us a programme was made on a community playgroup on the vast Leigh Park housing estate,[1] and another on teenagers in playgroups in nearby Portsmouth. Films of both were made for hiring.

Then came the *Open Door* programme, devised and directed by playgroup people, with a film of the playgroup sequences.[2] Women's programmes, panels, discussion groups and phone-ins include our members both nationally and regionally, and we are included in consultative groups discussing programmes for the under-fives and schools programmes.

There are still two major needs to be met.

1. There is a dichotomy between films for entertainment, and films for education. It seems to have escaped notice that parents (and grandparents) find children entertaining, and they could be drawn out of their unawareness of children by sensitive filming carefully directed and produced. This would mean that occasionally peak viewing time could be given to such a programme.

More programmes are needed that will show under-fives reacting naturally to a variety of situations. 'Points of View' is popular enough to enjoy peak viewing time; and 'Children Talking' has proved to be another winner. Could we not now

[1] *Your kids join you join.*
[2] *A playgroup of our own.*

have 'Children Playing', and allow adults to be entertained and educated at the same time?

2. Since playgroup courses are not yet established all over the country, and since even established tutors are not finding it easy to come in on playgroup wave-length, there is a need for televised tutoring on an extended scale. For example, five programmes would not be too many to show five different people telling stories to five different groups of children: it is not merely the art of telling a story that is needed, it is a chance to see what other people do and say when someone in the group interrupts the story.

The camera can let the audience in on live, and potentially disastrous situations. Just what does the competent story-teller do when Tracy announces loudly that she wants 'to wee', William decides to run his dinky car up and down the chair leg, and Horace interrupts to say that his dog is not a big black one but a little brown one with short legs?

5. *Films*

Playgroup courses revealed the need for a special type of teaching film. Many people enjoying courses are unable to read fluently, and often have an aversion to book learning; others read avidly but are unable to translate what they read into action when confronted with a group of real children. Language is often a barrier to real communication, especially such words as play, freedom, discipline, naughty, good. Many people have never been helped to think clearly and logically, but their senses of sight, hearing and touch are well developed in practical situations. Added to this diversity of learning patterns there is the added complication that most adults tend to think that children are smaller editions of themselves, and credit them with thoughts, feelings and desires that are replicas of their own.

Bearing this accumulation of experiences in mind, PPA devised an experimental series of teaching films. The first six were made by Images for Education Films Ltd, and shown to widely differing playgroup audiences. The reaction is more than encouraging, but it is clear that those who show them need to understand why they are made as they are:

(*a*) The films are not in colour. The largest audience for the film is likely to be mothers on playgroup courses, and almost all of them will be emotionally involved with the under-fives. A shot of a green-eyed, auburn-haired, freckle-faced child clad in olive green is likely to call forth the reaction, 'Oh, isn't he gorgeous!'

The aim of these films is to keep the emotional climate cool, to enable the mothers *to see what the children are doing.* Colour is likely to call forth their emotional reaction *to the children themselves.*

(*b*) The films are silent. The reasoning is the same: if the mothers hear an adult voice speaking to them, part of their attention will be diverted to listening. We want the whole of their attention to be directed to seeing, in the hope that the visual image will be strong enough to draw them into the child's world to the point where they begin to feel what these play experiences are meaning to the child.

(*c*) Each of the films deals with only one activity in order that the viewer shall have time to grasp exactly what children do when faced with clay, or dough, or water. It is not true that adults lose interest unless the camera darts from one place to another: on the contrary, the cry with most films is 'just when I was longing to know what he was going to do next the camera whisked on to something else'.

(*d*) Each film lasts only ten minutes. This is nothing to do with economy. The idea is to allow time for the film to be shown twice, with a period for discussion after each showing. Audience reaction shows that the strongest first impressions tend to be adult-centred.

'Why didn't they have aprons?'

'I didn't think they should have been allowed to have a knife.'

'We haven't got a table that size.'

'I noticed that the little chap who enjoyed it most didn't do his share of the clearing up.'

'I thought the clay was too hard.'

'I didn't like the way the clay was put on the table—we have ours...'

'We put chairs round our clay table.'

Playgroup people are so preoccupied comparing what the film playgroup does with what *they* do that the children are hardly noticed at all. All the queries must be dealt with fully for there is learning in discussing how it comes about that some playgroups find clay to be a clean enough activity for the children not to need overalls, whilst other groups find that they get filthy. Is it the clay? The children? The management?

After the adult-seeing has been discussed, it is then possible for them to begin to recall the children. Slowly, very slowly, child-centred images come back to them.

'They were terribly busy all the time, yet they didn't actually *do* anything.'

'They seemed just to love the feel of it.'

'Some were working hard with their hands, but their eyes were darting about all over the place.'

'I loved the way one boy had nearly finished piling huge lumps on top of each other, and then another began to give him minute pieces.'

'When the little chap put water on his hard clay, it only made the outside slippery; when the bigger girl did it she was able to work it in so that the whole lump became soft, and then she could do what she liked with it.'

At this point the film can be shown again, and this time they really 'see' the children, and are fascinated. Many parents confuse creativity with making things, but the children make it clear that the first vital stage is exploration and discovery.

What sort of playgroup should be filmed? It is too soon to say yet. Water play in a baby's bath may be taken to indicate that it is not necessary to aim any higher than this; an expensive water tray may discourage those who have to raise every penny by jumble sales; a carefully painted cottage tin bath may bring forth the despairing cry 'But we would never be able to store that!'

We have started from what we hope to be an inspirational point. The playgroup filmed was established about ten years ago by a nursery school teacher for her own children; there has

FOOTNOTE 1976

In 1976 The Churches Television and Radio Centre made two films in co-operation with us, *Parents in Playgroups* and *Country Children* (see Film List at back of book for address).

always been a mixture of privileged children and those who have been referred as being in special need; the premises are old, unattractive but large; the present playgroup leader is unqualified, but had helped in nursery schools for many years. Above all, this playgroup produces happy, adventurous, self-controlled, eager, reasonable, confident children: they are larger than life because of the love, trust and stimulation that exists between them, the playgroup leader and the mothers. Watchers may fairly disagree with this-and-that; but the children illustrate so clearly how all children learn by doing that it seemed justified to start with such a group.

6. *Toys and equipment*

Three developments are noted here.

Firstly, some old-established firms are now meeting the new demands of playgroups with integrity and imagination. Equipment is specially designed to slide under stages, hang from wall and ceiling hooks, stack flat in cupboards and passages and hold small items in stacked trays. Lack of funds is being countered by the production of some good, well-designed toys and equipment made in serviceable but cheaper materials, rather than in a cheaper version of the original material. Wooden toys and bricks are more often left with their natural grain, rather than plastered with transfers and letters of the alphabet.

Complaints are dealt with not just by a replacement but by redesigning at the production stage. One example of this was a climbing frame which included a platform that rested on the bars, steadied only by an inside stop; several energetic children managed to cause the platform to 'give' and slip down between the bars. A new version was designed in such a way that the platform clamps down safely with stops on both sides of the supporting bars.

Secondly, some firms are jumping on the bandwagon, and producing cheap and useless toys and equipment. Fortunately, fund raising is so much effort, and the disappointment is so great when the eagerly-awaited purchase proves to be unserviceable, that purchasers write to *Contact* as well as to the manufacturers. Those who have been bitten are not only shy, they take active steps to prevent other playgroup people from being similarly bitten.

Thirdly, many firms are offering easy terms; the well-established firms, whose prices are high but whose goods are proven, advertise this fact in an unsensational manner, and those who are going to buy this sort of equipment tend to think carefully about it. Other firms use the hard sell technique, and the 'Why-wait? Have it now!' temptation is aimed at the very people who should be most wary of this approach to playgroups.

It is the families most tempted by the tally-man who need to experience the satisfaction of raising the money before spending it; it is the families who are quickly moved by impulse who are most likely to find that a hastily started playgroup folds up in the first year. Who is going to pay the bills? What is to be done with the equipment?

This is why PPA branches try to build up a stock of big equipment to lend out to new playgroups. If the playgroup founders, the equipment is taken back into the branch and lent to the next applicant; if the playgroup flourishes money will be raised to buy their own equipment, and when it arrives the triumphant mothers can return the lent equipment to the branch —to which they are, by then, happily attached in a creative bond of friendship.

7. Books

Children's books have surely never been better, but there is an alarming increase in review copies of so-called 'books for playgroups' being sent to PPA's office. Occasionally a book is so good that one wishes every playgroup in the country had a copy to be lent to every new generation of parent. But sometimes a book is so wide of the mark that one wishes it had never been written, particularly as these are the ones that one suspects will sell all too well.

The damaging books are those giving directions for the making of unlimited small things. The author usually explains that they are simple enough to be made with a minimum of adult help and guidance, and every page shows exactly how you make a potato hedgehog, a rug wool daisy, an egg box caterpillar, a cheese box clock, a cork horse, a toilet roll 'Dougal', a king's crown, etc. The writers of these books have not understood how nature decrees that children learn by 'doing', and that what is 'done' is rarely of importance to the child—unless the adult makes it a means of winning approval. They have not understood that a playgroup should be a place where children are allowed freedom-to-discover. They have not understood that what is done under the watchful eyes of playgroup mothers is taken into the home and repeated, and that children need to be imaginative, not repetitive. They have not understood that mothers constantly and anxiously compare what their child does with what other children of a similar age do—and as soon as everyone is making the same thing the comparisons can be quite misleading and very damaging indeed to the child-mother relationship.

They have not understood that a mother invariably calls children 'good' or 'clever' when they have done what they have been told to do, and that this concept of goodness is not always valid, neither does this type of copying indicate cleverness. They have not understood that they are setting the rat-race in motion, because all too soon the mothers will greet the children with, 'Haven't you made anything today?' and the children begin to learn that something tangible is expected before you can win adult approval. Saddest of all, they have not understood that the very playgroup leaders who will thankfully buy the books and use them are those who are so insecure that they do not dare to visit other playgroups or go on courses which would enable them to run a real playgroup.

There are many delightful picture books to be found, and many equally delightful illustrated stories with varying quantities of text. But there seems to be a gap between the two types of book. A publisher is collaborating with PPA to produce a series of books that tell stories without words. The new series takes a simple theme, such as 'Going Shopping', and the child can turn over twenty pages and 'read' the story from the sequence of pictures. In the early stages this will probably be an experience shared with an adult, which will give both the joy of togetherness and the stimulation of conversation. In time the child will be able to 'read' the story for himself, and it is to be hoped that over-anxious mothers will begin to understand that this is really a pre-reading stage. They consistently doubt the valid pre-reading experience offered by looking at, and handling, books.

The books are inexpensive, with the cost kept down to the

minimum by selling direct through advertisements in *Contact* and *Under-5*. Many of the mothers for whom *Under-5* is intended are used to purchasing through the postal order services, and it is hoped that they will cut out the coupon and send off their postal order for the usual reasons—a desire to have something to look forward to, and a desire to get in a tangible form something, anything, that might help to fill the intangible void. It is hoped that the eagerly awaited packet will give real pleasure both to the mother and her child, and that it might lead to a slow build-up of books in the home.

The first books are clearly and firmly marked 'three to five years'; no doubt some mothers will say that their two-year-olds enjoyed them, and that they are insulting to a five-year-old's intelligence. We know from experience that many five-year-olds have never looked at books, and it is for these children particularly that the new series is planned. It would be unthinkable to mark them for 'two-year-olds or deprived five-year-olds'. We also know from experience that children need to regress from time to time, and if a perfectly normal, happy, intelligent five-year-old child happens to be enjoying a book intended for 'two to three years', then the mother in the playgroup can become anxious lest her child is backward and 'won't get on all right' when he goes to school.

It cannot be over-emphasized that the presence of mothers in the playgroup alters the whole approach to what is suitable or unsuitable. In some ways it would be easier to keep them out, but it is infinitely more rewarding to keep them in, though this demands as much sensitivity to their needs as to the needs of the children.

In 1972 Collins produced *Mother's Help, for busy mothers and playgroup leaders*. Eleven contributors, all experienced in different ways with children's activities, wrote to share their particular enthusiasms with mothers: toy making, co-operative cooking, living things, party giving, dressing-up, art and creativity, electronic toys, telling stories, making music, the child in bed, and starting a playgroup.

In 1974 *The Penguin Book of Playgroups* by Joyce Lucas and Vivienne McKennell appeared. Both write with personal experience of being in playgroups and tutoring playgroup courses. That same year *Playtime Stories* was published as a Young

Puffin Original. It was written by Joyce Donoghue, mother of five, who, at the time of writing, was vice-chairman of PPA. It was not just loyalty that sold 50,000 copies in two years: the stories stirred ideas in those who read them aloud for their story value. In 1975 Faber produced *Playgroups, a practical approach* by Hilde Jarecki, who pioneered so valiantly as the first professional adviser responsible for organizing the development of the Inner London playgroups between 1964 and 1972.

Students continue to write to tell us that they are writing a thesis on playgroups, and asking us to direct them to literature on the subject. It is good to have a growing number of books written from first-hand experience of playgroups—but we always put the writers in touch with their nearest playgroup branch, stressing that reading is no substitute for seeing, listening and doing.

Chapter 10

Playgroup courses

Playgroup courses were called into being by the playgroup mothers almost as soon as the movement began, and in trying to meet their needs much has been learned. Society has become more aware of the fact that if children are streamed they tend to become what they are presumed to be: a D-stream child expects nothing of himself because he has already been presumed to have little capacity either to give or to receive. Yet we are in danger of putting parents into categories which may have the same effect on them as streaming the children.

It is essential for the healthy, happy vitality of the playgroup movement that all mothers, all playgroup leaders, all helpers, whatever their background and ability, shall be seen as people. The implications of this are not as obvious as they seem, but they must be clearly understood before anyone sets out to plan a playgroup course based on a syllabus and a book list related to the needs and development of the under-fives.

Playgroup courses draw people from a wide cross-section of the population, and most of the students are mothers who are naturally emotionally involved with their own children. But although the students are brought together by their common experiences of motherhood, they are at the same time divided by the widely differing patterns of thought and behaviour which result from their varied upbringings and environments.

No one should be asked to speak to playgroup students unless she has visited playgroups; and anyone undertaking the tutoring of the major part of a course should have seen playgroups typifying the various groupings outlined in Chapter 1. Only by understanding each situation as it exists at the beginning of a course is it possible to work effectively towards something better.

A playgroup course has to do two things simultaneously. First, to help students in the simple practicalities of *presenting* the appropriate activities; and the much less simple practicalities of *managing* each activity once the children have arrived in the carefully prepared playroom. Second, to enable students, without intensifying their guilt and anxiety, to modify their attitudes. In this respect a good playgroup course must achieve the paradox of both boosting confidence, and of arousing a proper humility as we come to see that all too often we impose patterns of behaviour and activity on our children that are derived from our own false certainties rather than the needs of children. The balance of these paradoxes is important, for neither over-confidence nor a loss of confidence is desirable.

WHO SHOULD BE ACCEPTED ON A COURSE?

Courses should be open for all: *there should be no selection or rejection.* This means that on any course there may not only be people from widely different cultural backgrounds, with widely different academic abilities, but also people with very different connections with the playgroup, varying from playgroup leaders, regular helpers and rota mothers to those who mistakenly call themselves 'just mothers'.

The old rigidities of academic streaming have no place on a playgroup course: it *is* possible to teach everyone together, given the right tutor. It is a mistake to segregate playgroup leaders and 'just mothers', for each needs to understand the difficulties of the other. Again, given the right tutor, the embarrassment of letting-down the playgroup leader in the eyes of the 'just mothers' does not arise. One of the first jobs of a tutor is to help people to see that neither playgroup leaders nor mothers are right or wrong, it is a matter of understanding mutual difficulties and needs in order that situations may be handled to the benefit of all concerned.

SHOULD THERE BE WRITTEN EXAMINATIONS?

No. The proof of what we are trying to achieve lies essentially

133

in the living realm of human growth and relationships. In order to know whether or not we are succeeding as tutors we must visit our students in their playgroups to see:

if they can present and manage a full range of play activities;
if they understand how to help the children towards self-discipline;
if they understand and respond to the essential dignity of children and childhood;
if they know the difference between talking to and talking with children;
if they recognize the moment when exploration has passed over the borderline into silliness;
if they are able to say 'no' at the right moment, and mean it;
if they are able to keep their own emotions in check as they cope with potentially difficult situations without reference to anything other than the child's need at the moment;
if they can create an atmosphere of happiness, stability and serenity;
if they can tell a story, and cope with interruptions in such a way that the story is not spoiled for anyone else;
if they can enjoy rhymes and finger plays with the children;
if they can make other mothers feel wanted and needed;
if they can handle difficult children in front of their mothers without the mother being made to lose face;
if they can delegate responsibility on every possible occasion in order that both children and adults shall continue to grow in responsibility.

How can any of these things be tested on paper? Before anyone points out that not even a three-year training could be guaranteed to achieve all this, let me add that I have met so-called uneducated mothers who were able, even before a good playgroup course, to fulfil naturally all the above 'ifs', with the exception of the first one. *It is easier to help such a mother to acquire the skills of presentation and management of equipment than it is to help a highly educated and academically able mother to be a good playgroup leader if she lacks the vital ability to relate warmly to other people.*

SHOULD COURSES BE GRADED?

Yes. Broadly speaking the needs of playgroup people fall into three phases: What? How? and Why?

1. *The What? stage*

This needs to be satisfied before the playgroup starts. The dominant questions are: What do I do to start? What sums of money are involved? What shall we buy? What do we make? What can we improvise? What do children need to play with? What exactly do you do to mix paint, fingerpaint, dough? What keeps clay from going hard? What arrangement of the room is best? What do you do about planning the time, or don't you? What do you do about music if you can't play the piano? Or stories if you are afraid to tell them? What sort of dolls' clothes and dressing-up clothes do we need?

2. *The How? stage*

This needs to come after there has been a period of practical work in the playgroup. A host of questions now arise as to how to cope with the combination of children and activities. The centre of attention still tends to be the equipment rather than the children; the effort involved in raising the funds, making and improvising is still very intense.

The next questions tend to be: How do you stop children mixing up the puzzles? spilling the sand? mixing the sand and water together? taking water into the home corner and making everything wet? interrupting a story? spoiling music? throwing things? shouting? How do you help a shy child to separate from his mother? How do you cope with a bossy child? a child who takes things? How do you cope when a child wants to paint or sit on the tricycle all morning? How do you cope with boys who only want to make gun noises? or the rising fives who are bored by everything?

Students want practical work, demonstrations, suggestions based on practical experience, and a chance to discuss their own thoughts and feelings. Practical work needs to come first. Discussion is needed throughout (but beware of discussion groups where the blind lead the blind, and so reinforce everything that you were hoping they might come to relinquish).

135

Theory needs to be interwoven with both the practical work and the discussion.

3. *The Why? stage*

After further experience of working with the children, there usually comes the stage where people have learned to cope with many different types of child and various patterns of behaviour.

At this point they are sufficiently free of their own doubts and anxieties to be deeply interested in the children, and the next wave of questions is along the lines of: Why are children who are so good at home so often wild in the playgroup? Why do some children stick at one thing so long when others dash from thing to thing? Why do some children seem to take a delight in upsetting other children? Why do some children defy you every time you ask them to do something? Why are some children so afraid of getting dirty? Why do some children take so long to join in? Why do they listen when you explain that they mustn't be unkind, and then go and do exactly the same thing again?

Advanced theory is often asked for, but it can be a trap for the unwary. Of what use is it if a student is enabled to talk for hours about Piaget and his theories if she has understood the practical implications so little that the first time she catches a four-year-old biting a three-year-old she delivers a moral lecture full of concepts such as kindness, fairness and goodness?

Tutors embarking on theory need to be very sure that their students are able to go into the playgroup and bring back living examples of the speech and behaviour that illustrate these theories: without this proof of real learning it is all too easy for students to enjoy a dangerous intellectual one-upmanship.

An increasing number of playgroup people ask for more advanced courses. PPA is reluctant to instigate these for the following reasons.

1. There is such a constant waiting list for courses that tutors are needed to disseminate the earlier stages of learning as widely as possible. Extra-advanced courses would take tutors away from the field where they are most needed.

2. Some of those who wish to go on really need to go back to first principles of observation of materials, children and adults in the playgroup.

136

3. If courses become too advanced the word will get around and the so-called '11-plus failures' will either be afraid to embark on courses at all, or they will only dare to go on the first one or two, and will feel failures yet again as they hold back from joining those at the upper end of the learning scale.

These students are encouraged to go on to various specialist courses, with or without a qualification in view, and it is gratifying to note how many playgroup people go on to do teacher training—still more gratifying to be told so often by the principals of such colleges that playgroup mothers are the best teacher-material that it has ever been their pleasure to train.

No one should feel debarred from progressive learning; but the primary function of playgroup courses is to lay solid foundations so that children can learn through play, and mothers can learn from children playing, and from each other.

WHAT IS THE IDEAL SITUATION FOR A PLAYGROUP COURSE?

The ideal situation for a playgroup course is one where these facilities are available:

1. Ample scope for everyone to handle clay, mix dough, mix paint, try out painting and fingerpainting, set up water play and interest corners, make puppets and dressing-up clothes.

2. An opportunity to set out a playgroup, moving around activities and large equipment until the best possible placing has been found for that particular room.

3. Facilities for coffee, or lunch, if it is a day course. This break is important, as it enables people to talk over the first part of the session and to come back to the second half in the knowledge that they are all in the same boat. And it is here that they begin to form personal friendships (we underestimate their basic shyness, and it has been known for courses to end without anyone finding out the name or address of anyone else).

4. Facilities for an adjacent playgroup, so that people can link theory and practice all the way along the line.

The composition of this playgroup is important. If it is only a collection of under-fives brought by the playgroup mothers then there is never the settled feeling of continuity that is the essence of a good playgroup. The playgroup needs to be an accepted part of the locality, with regular children coming in throughout the week; but when the register is being compiled, enough places have to be left on playgroup course days so that mothers who have three- and four-year-olds can bring them. The regular children who will also be there create the atmosphere which helps the once-a-week children to settle in happily. It helps if mothers on the course introduce their children to the playgroup a week or two before the course begins. It is difficult to concentrate if the playgroup leader is constantly calling you out to reassure your child, and it is equally difficult to pay attention if you are cuddling a distressed child on your lap.

5. A local nursery school and several nearby playgroups where students may go to observe. These playgroups need playgroup leaders who will also be willing to allow students to practise story-telling, music, the presentation of fingerpainting, or the introduction of a special talk-point (such as a guinea pig, or a violin). It is very much easier to practise in someone else's playgroup, for nothing claims your attention save the job in hand—and most people find it easier to tell a story in a quiet spot among friendly, matter-of-fact strangers than in front of personal friends who tend to make the story-teller acutely self-conscious.

Chapter 11

Tutors

Playgroup people have begun to realize that their use of the word tutor is misleading. *In playgroup parlance tutor means the one constant leader, demonstrator, friend, who will be appointed to take each session of the course.* Experience shows that insecure or rigid mothers are unable to let go of their prejudices and misconceptions unless they can form a warm and trusting relationship with such a tutor. This only comes about after weeks of listening to her answering questions: no one is willing to ask the revealing questions until she is certain that they will be answered with tolerance, understanding and common sense.

Any course having such a tutor is fortunate, and the chances are that she has learned by trial and error over a long period. If she decides to introduce a visiting specialist for, say, music, then she attends with her as a matter of courtesy: but it is also important to sense the reaction of the students to the guest speaker. Sometimes it is immediately obvious that she is exactly right; sometimes it is clear that the briefing has been inadequate, but the outlook is hopeful; occasionally it is a disaster, and the wisest course will be to thank her, making a mental reservation about repeating the invitation. Where a guest is immediately right the bond with the class is instantaneous, and from then on the tutor usually feels able to enter into an easy relationship whereby the two of them do not need to double-up on subsequent sessions, or the guest may become intrigued and ask to be allowed to join the rest of the course to find out what it is all about. New tutors have been found in this way.

Most courses begin in the nature of an experiment, and a large team of willing individuals is formed. In these cases it is imperative to employ a constant link, call her chairman, or what you will. This type of course often leads to a great deal of overlapping: because of the natural tendency of mothers (particularly) to hear what they were expecting or wanting to hear, someone has to be there each week in order to cope with the following week's questions which begin 'I've been thinking about what X said last week and. . .' Sometimes such a chairman will sit through several courses, until she suddenly realizes what it is that the students need; furthermore, she is prepared to take on the job herself, and does. Many of these links are playgroup people, often qualified appropriately, but they had not thought to offer their services previously for fear of not being good enough. They thought that lecturers were wanted, and came to see for themselves that this is not the case.

WHO ARE THE IDEAL TUTORS FOR A PLAYGROUP COURSE?

Perhaps the ideal tutor would be:

1. Knowledgeable about child development, and experienced in working with groups of normal under-fives, so that the usual ninety per cent of questions beginning, 'What do you do with a child when . . .?' can be answered from the depth and breadth of that personal experience.

2. Parent orientated. One retired nursery school teacher put it in a nutshell when she said, 'I always had a close relationship with all my mothers. But, you know, looking back I can see that I never really saw them as *people*—I just wanted to help them for the children's sake, rather than their own.'

There is a world of difference between befriending parents so that they shall be better towards their children, and identifying with them as people who are struggling to find their own identity and happiness, just as we are ourselves.

3. Knowledgeable about playgroups. Playgroup people know in a minute whether or not we have visited playgroups, just as they know if we have visited only one playgroup, for we give ourselves away in the self-conscious display of our knowledge of the particular storage difficulties of that particular group, or the particular layout of that particular hall. Only when we have visited many playgroups do we really appreciate their difficulties and triumphs.

4. Knowledgeable about people. Not the superficial knowledge that enables us to say 'Black hair, back row—a know-all', 'Little blonde with glasses—neurotic', 'Lass with ginger hair—stands out a mile', 'Plump, pink jumper—going to be a bore about her own children'. It needs to be the sort of understanding that grasps early on in the course just what different people are likely to be doing in their playgroups; just how it comes about that they are doing it; and along what particular line their minds are likely to work, in order that we can try to draw them carefully through the thicket of their misconceptions.

5. Generous enough to spot potential tutors from among the students, and to enjoy helping them to grow into new tutors. Many tutors fulfil all these idealistic hopes, but most of us grope slowly and clumsily through our various stages of learning. The point of outlining an ideal is to make it clear that academic qualifications alone are not enough.

HOW CAN TUTORS USED TO ACADEMIC STREAMING COME TO TERMS WITH THIS NEW SITUATION?

The ability of those on the courses, both to receive and to give back, can be there but the different backgrounds sometimes render communication difficult at first. A playgroup course tutor has constantly to ask herself, 'How can I convey professional truth in such a way that it is understood by everyone?' Perhaps it comes down to the fundamental level of 'Can I impart the professional knowledge that I have and they need, without using a single word of my own professional jargon?'

Many of us have tutored in other spheres, and have learned to judge ourselves so that we know even during a session whether we are teaching well or teaching badly. What we have had to learn during our playgroup apprenticeship is that it is perfectly possible for us to feel that we have taught well, only to discover when visiting the playgroups afterwards that we have not apparently taught anything at all. The one redeeming feature is our certainty that during the course people grow in stature before our very eyes: once perception is sparked it flares into life and attitudes begin to change, judgments soften and comparisons come in shades of grey instead of black and white. And the anonymous jottings at the end of a course hardly ever vary: 'I understand children so much better'; 'I understand myself so much better'; 'I am much more tolerant with other mothers'; 'When my own children are difficult I don't fly off the handle; I ask myself "Why?"'

But a change in attitudes is not always enough to change the playgroup which is already in full swing and has the force of habit behind it. Where did we go wrong? Too much talk and not enough do: playgroup people need practical work.

FINDING TUTORS

This is probably the greatest difficulty of all. No matter how gifted someone may be with children, or as the possessor of specialist knowledge, if he or she cannot relate well with the students nothing happens. Yet the students' reactions are not always a reliable guide either: 'Tuesday was awful' may mean 'She knew her stuff about children all right, but she spoke to us as though we were four-years-old too'; 'She knew all about six-year-olds but she hadn't a clue about our age group'; 'She got our backs up, her own children just couldn't have been that marvellous'; 'She couldn't control the interruptions, and X went on and on about her own child'; 'It was all theory, and every time we asked a practical question she said she couldn't answer it without knowing the particular child, the parents, the home background. That's all very well, but we've still got to do *something* about the child who bites.'

Most tutors can sense hostility, but it is not often that there is anyone on a course mature enough to offer constructive help. Many tutors who begin badly can, and do, learn to come in on the right wave-length. *Briefing beforehand is infinitely preferable to grumbling afterwards.*

On the other hand, 'Tuesday was marvellous' may mean 'The doctor was an absolute dish'—in their enthusiasm they overlook the fact that he did not deal with splinters down nails, beads up noses, gravel in grazes, sand in eyes, and cuts that look as though they might need stitching. Or 'She saw eye to eye with me about everything'—alas their eyes may have been on distressing targets such as six weeks' rehearsal for the end of term concert, which has no place in a playgroup. Or 'She's got an absolutely inexhaustible fund of ideas for things children could make'—it is incredibly difficult to help people to see that doing and making are appropriate to quite different stages of development. It cannot be said too often, or too clearly, that playgroup children should not be encouraged by adults to make an end-product. They should be free to do for the sake of doing. A decision to make something is rare in the under-fives; and when it comes about it will be a deeply personal endeavour, nothing to do with mass-production.

Many NNEB tutors in education and nursery school teachers are invaluable; sometimes infant teachers are very much on the right wavelength, and already have helpful contacts with the local playgroups; often the local area organizer of PPA is the right person to carry a course; sometimes local specialists have the ability to inspire students in a particular field—music, pre-school painting, nature, storytelling, woodwork: always there are playgroup people with much to offer.

But it is now clear that PPA must continue to produce tutors from experienced playgroup people in every type of community. *No existing training sets out to prepare people to relate to children in front of their parents in such a way that the parent gains new insight without being diminished in her own eyes, or in the eyes of her child and her neighbours.*

We also learn that 'resource groups' are needed to complement the tutors' courses now well established in several areas.

DIFFICULTIES THAT FACE TUTORS

1. Most playgroup leaders are mothers, and are therefore emotionally involved with anything to do with the under-fives. If the tutor explains a facet of children or childhood that is new and disturbing to a mother she may well recoil or lash out. It takes time to realize that it is not a personal attack, but the whiplash of sudden panic lest the child has been damaged for life by this lack of knowledge.

2. Many people on the course have come hoping for Ten Quick Tips, and it is disconcerting to find that there is no such thing.

143

3. Most people come to receive confirmation that what they are doing is right. It is therefore a shock to discover that their right is someone else's wrong; and an even greater shock to discover that the tutor is not going to take sides.

4. Most mothers find it difficult to see life through a child's eyes.

Possibly this is where the playgroup courses are so valuable to mothers as people. For years they have literally been responsible for their children's lives, and have had to decide what was best for the children—an extra woolly, more food, a dose of magnesia, time for bed, clean socks, new shoes. On and on it goes, quite rightly. But unless help is forthcoming to break this pattern of 'I-know-best', the parent-child relationship is heading for trouble.

Quite often it falls to the tutor to be the breaking stone, and she must understand this if she is not going to engage in a pointless verbal battle with a desire to win. When a mother says vehemently, 'I don't think that children should . . .', 'I think they ought to . . .', 'It isn't right that . . .', 'I don't agree with . . .', 'I . . .', 'I . . .', the particular issue in question is infinitely less important than the handling of the confrontation itself. An understanding tutor can help a mother to see things from the child's point of view, without losing face herself.

TWO 'TIPS' FOR TUTORS

1. Clear the air about certificates right at the start of the course, so that there can be no possible misunderstanding. A certificate of attendance is usually given—sufficiently discreet not to tempt people to frame it and hang it on the wall— stating that X has attended so many sessions. It will have no national validity except to indicate that X cared enough about her playgroup to seek knowledge.

Playgroup courses are improving all the time, and in some areas where local authorities formerly insisted that playgroup leaders had to have previous qualifications, there is now a willingness to allow them to start on the strength of having attended a local playgroup course. But this is not a 'qualification'. Experience indicates that the attitude of the tutor is all-important in seeing that everyone starts the course happily, in the knowledge that it merely sets out to support, enlighten and help.

2. At the last session of a course, without previous warning, give out sheets of paper and say, in effect, 'You needn't put your name on it, and I don't know your handwriting, so will you just jot down what *you* really got out of the course, and anything else you'd like to say.' If these comments are done at home they will be laboured and polite, and pointlessly stereotyped. If questions are set out for them to answer, or tick, then the thoughts are not their own. If we ask for criticism they are likely to write in negative terms (because they think of it as a negative word). But if we ask for 'What *you've* really got out of it', then the response is positive, original, and immensely valuable.

The comments are illuminating, 'Relief that most people have to arbitrate between husbands and children', 'Surprise at how clever children really are sometimes when at first you thought they'd just been naughty', 'Relief to find that on the whole I haven't been too bad a mother', 'Now I do things because I understand, and not just because everybody says it's the right thing to do', 'Excitement at suddenly finding I begin to understand why children do things'. But it takes courage to swallow, 'I wish you hadn't let some people monopolize you', 'I wish you'd started on time and not waited for late-comers, we make a real effort to get here on time, and then we waste the first ten minutes', 'I wish you hadn't let the discussions get so woolly'.

IS THERE ANY POSSIBILITY OF A NATIONALLY RECOGNIZED COURSE?

Yes, but it is some way off yet for several reasons:

1. PPA is still learning, and the simple truth is that a course aimed only at improving the standard of play fails to produce the desired result in the playgroup. The twin aim must be to help

FOOTNOTE 1976

In 1975 PPA produced *Guidelines for a Foundation Course*, price £1·10, available from PPA, Alford House, Aveline Street, London SE11 5DH.

mothers for their own sake, in order that their understanding of both motherhood and childhood is raised to the point where being a mother is rightly seen to be creative, exciting, challenging and infinitely worthwhile—in spite of the physical and nervous exhaustion that is all too often predominant. The playgroups improve in proportion to their *real* understanding: it is the quality of tutoring that counts, not the content of a syllabus.

2. There are too few centres which are able to offer adequate facilities for practical work: for visiting nursery schools and several playgroups for observation; and for making provision for tutors to visit the students to see them working with children.

3. There are too few tutors who understand what is needed. And those who do are being seriously overworked, sometimes to the detriment of their own full-time jobs.

4. No quick and slick method can enlarge the tutoring force. One way to create tutors seems to be for good existing tutors to foster and encourage potential tutors from among the students of former courses. Such people need to attend the course a second time. The first time they attend to learn for their own benefit; the second time it is to watch the interaction between students and tutor, and to listen to the tutor answering questions—for it is during the answering of questions that most is probably learned.[1]

IS THERE A SET SYLLABUS FOR PLAYGROUP COURSES?

No, not yet, but for some years past PPA has offered notes for the guidance of new tutors. Many areas are running courses that are very valuable to the students attending them, even though they cannot yet be offered all that is needed. A set syllabus at this stage would cut short new thinking, which is still in a highly creative state. Yet some guide lines must be offered. Chapter 12 enlarges on the content of playgroup courses.

[1] By 1974 there were 28 experimental playgroup tutors' courses in existence, and a conference was held to enable representatives from each course to meet together to share learning and thinking.

IS THERE A BOOK LIST?

PPA has one based on the recommendation of those who have tutored playgroup courses for the last five or six years. It is carefully planned to meet many needs.

Chapter 12

The content of playgroup courses

PRACTICAL WORK

The constant cry is for 'More practical work'. The sort of practical work that is needed and greatly appreciated relates to the presentation of activities. Since this field of tutoring is still so new, many tutors are finding it difficult to discover just what it is that playgroup people need.

Water

Sometimes the water play is in evidence, but it consists of two inches of water in the bottom of a baby bath, and a vast collection of plastic containers, rusty motor boats, cups and saucers, balls, jugs, yogurt pots, funnels, bottles, jars, lids, Uncle Tom Cobley and all—with a mystified playleader saying, 'Everyone says children should have water play, so we always do, but we never find they're interested in it, what do other people find?'

Clearly it is necessary to present water play in detail on courses, not only to show how to protect the floor, and how to choose the right number and combination of objects to put into (or beside) the bath or tank or tray, but also to offer suggestions as to the possible reaction of both children and parents.

This is the constant extra factor in playgroup tutoring— the parents are involved (if not always in the playgroup itself), and they are *emotionally* involved. The average mother truly thinks that wet feet can lead to a chill, that the chill can lead to pneumonia, and pneumonia can lead to death. (She probably knows perfectly well that this fear is silly—but the knowledge does nothing to alleviate the fear.) So we must help the supervisors to present water play in such a way that the children do not get wet; but we must also bring out this question of irrational fears—these playgroup mothers recognize it in an instant, and there is a gale of laughter. But in the laughter there is relief at finding how prone we all are to these feelings; there is also an immediate pooling of ideas for keeping feet dry—adult gumboots cut down, to accommodate the child's slippered feet; sponge rubber sewn round the hem of the water apron; a plastic apron that descends to the ground; a water tray let into a table with an eight-inch formica surround; a plastic bag for each foot held under the knee by a garter. Ideas, good and bad, flood in, and the tutor learns as much as anybody.

Mother involvement also makes it necessary to deal in some detail with the question of mopping up. Housewives have, over the years, developed their own techniques and standards: some mothers rush for a cloth at the first spot, others wait until the floor is awash and then go in search of the caretaker's rather murky mop and zinc bucket. Discussion and even demonstration is needed as the group considers what is inevitable, what is unreasonable, what is deliberate, and what is truly innocent overspilling: and when and how it is coped with, and by whom.

None of this is easy for a tutor, at first. Most of us are all too conscious of the fact that some of the students are more intelligent than we are, and we are reluctant to insult their intelligence, even though we suspect that some people need help at a very fundamental level. The answer seems to be that however highly qualified people may be, *we must assume nothing*. It all has to be spelled out. And the difficulty lies in doing it in such a way that no one feels insulted.

As an opening gambit 'Now, let us first consider the floor covering!' will not do. By trial and error we learn that it is better to say 'Before we go on to water play, tell me what you all do about protecting floors—do you find that plastic sheeting gets dangerously slippery?' Everyone can wade in with suggestions and intelligent comparison; and those who had never thought of covering the floor at all can recover from the shock in silence, and learn without revealing their ignorance to anyone.

149

Sand

This needs the same degree of discussion and demonstration, including help on the sweeping up. Sometimes the sand escapes far beyond the confines of the floor covering, and the final sweep round over the floor boards yields a plentiful supply of dust, fluff and bits of paper, etc. which are put back into the sand tray. Mother involvement is relevant here, too. The economy of using swept-up sand is not just one of money, for the sand has to be collected; and someone has to make the effort and find the time to organize an already full day to include a trip to the nearest depot supplying washed sand. (Some have not been warned about unwashed sand, and are horrified to find clothes stained orange.) It is the sheer fag of doing this that prompts the rather grubby economy: understandable as lack of money and energy may be, standards of cleanliness and presentation must be kept high.

Clay

Adults often have inbuilt attitudes towards clay which affect their attitudes towards the children. First the students need to use clay themselves, and to discover how widely their own reactions to it differ. They need to know where to get it, what it costs, how to prepare the powdered clay, how to judge the water content of natural clay, how to store clay, how to reclaim clay that has dried rock-hard during the holidays. They all need to refresh their memories, to have a chance to re-learn or to learn for the first time the pleasure of clay as a material. Only then are they really receptive to the idea of offering it to the children; but even this step needs to be guided, for in the early stages of playgroup work most people find it terribly hard to learn *from* the children—the idea is so firmly established in our culture that adults teach children. It takes time for the habit of observation to be established, but it is from the children that these students begin to learn. We tutors can go on saying that children rarely set out to make anything, and hardly ever want or need an end-product—and no one really believes us. But it comes home when an observation reads, 'I asked him what he was making and he said, "I don't know. I haven't looked yet."'

150

Dough

The same stages need to be experienced as for clay. The child's point of view really comes over when an observation reads, 'Clare looked at the lump of dough on the empty table and said, "Can I have pastry?" She must have thought that pastry was the name for the dough, rolling pin, cutters and patty tins all together.'

Not until people have made dough, and have also handled other people's dough made from a different recipe, do they begin to sense its possibilities. It is not unusual for the summing-up of the session to take place with everyone sitting peacefully working a lump of dough in her hands as she joins in the discussion.

Personal attitudes come through the observations as clearly as the children's development. One 'difficult' child was given a great lump of senna-brown dough, which occupied him for a whole morning. 'I've never heard such a dirty laugh as his when he held it aloft and watched it drop!' A watching mother was deeply shocked, and walked away. But the child 'has been no trouble ever since'. It would be silly to pretend that this is the answer for all aggressive or inhibited children, but a significant number of playgroup leaders have found it to be so for certain children.

Parental attitudes also come over clearly in one batch of observations, showing that children in several playgroups discovered pattern-making by lying on the lump of dough to flatten it. Various children sat up to see imprints of buttons, ribbed corduroy, cable stitch pullovers or belt buckles (dough is clean, no clothes were spoiled) and with one exception they said joyfully, 'I've made a pattern.' The exception hadn't yet reached this stage of development, and he looked at his dough with bewilderment and said, 'There's marks on it!' The reactions of the playgroup leaders varied from 'I soon put a stop to that!' to 'I'm sure I ought to have stopped them, but they were so excited, and I felt they were really learning something as they went on to try out nose prints, knuckle prints, elbow prints, knee prints—and finally foot prints.' In the ensuing discussion it was agreed that there was a moment when learning ended, and 'just being silly' started, and one playgroup leader added 'I let my learning go too far, and suddenly they were throwing lumps of dough into the water tray.'

Most people find it difficult to steer a course between freedom and licence, and tutors need to be very much on the ball in order to save face for those who suddenly see that their rigidity was not as right as they had assumed, and for those who were once so gaily confident that chucking it about was free play.

Home corner

The words 'Wendy House' are still in general circulation, and equipment and toy catalogues keep alive this idea by their pictures of attractive miniature houses that are so exactly the adults' idea of what children would love. Certainly, some children love them as hidey holes; or enjoy popping in, shutting the door and laughing at the others through the windows; or will 'attack' them with guns or improvised fireman's hoses. But such miniature homes offer none of the opportunities for imaginative play that a group of children need. Better, by far, a large home corner bounded by screens or even rows of chairs.

The discussion, planning, and making of dolls' clothes, dressing-up clothes, equipment, etc. to prepare a home corner offer rich opportunities to understand more of child development. And until all our practical work is shot through with child development we shall continue to have expensive empty little houses or, alternatively, the curtained-off square of the hall filled with beds that are too small for the dolls, dolls' clothes that fit no doll properly, a crumpled pile of cast-off adults' clothes that pass for dressing-up clothes, and odd cups and saucers that match neither in colour or size; or a home corner so superbly equipped that it offers no scope at all for imaginative play.

The explanation as to why children want to *be* mothers and fathers (not play at mothers and fathers) usually resolves several difficulties straight away—notably the anxiety of fathers that if their sons want to dress up in women's clothes and pretend to be mothers, could they be potential homosexuals? Once it is understood that children need to find out what it feels like to be someone else, and to try out roles traditionally adopted by the opposite sex, then one of the purposes of the home corner becomes obvious. But think what opportunities can be added. If they have plastic coffee cups and saucers in different colours they can progress from grabbing any old cup and any old saucer, to making a deliberate choice of a matching cup and saucer. If they have knitted dolls' underclothes and satin dresses and velvet coats, they can feel the difference with their fingers. If dolls' clothes and dressing-up clothes have huge buttons for little fingers, fiddly hooks and eyes for more able fingers, then these skills are learned incidentally as the children play. If some dolls' clothes fasten on 'the boys' side' then left-handed children can learn these skills more easily.

Playgroup people need help in knowing how to keep imagination alive, and what to offer in order to stimulate it still further. How to provide opportunities for learning about size, shape, colour, number, the skills of dressing and undressing; and, of *great* importance, the management of the inevitable moment when the roused imaginations say, 'I know! Let's go and bath the baby in the water tank!' or, 'You go and get the scissors, and we'll be hairdressing ladies.'

As tutors, we must be very careful to foresee where our explanations and examples are going to lead our students. We are arousing their imagination and enthusiasm—but we must know what is likely to happen in their home corners as a result, and what the outcome is likely to be. What will the children do? How can the playgroup leader cope with the situation? *And what will be the effect on the other mothers in the playgroup?* What does a playgroup leader do when a mother sees the children remove a doll's knickers and examine the anatomy with deep interest or suggestive giggles, and promptly orders them out of the home corner because they are being naughty or rude? What does she do when two children squash into a bed together, and a mother says anxiously, 'Is it all right? Can it lead to anything?' What does she do when a mother breaks the boundary between the child's fantasy world and reality by going into the fantasy herself? We all accept and 'eat' imaginary cakes and sausages—but what is the effect on the child if we say, 'How lovely! I can see the sultanas, can you? Look at this lovely big one on the top!' Child development is very relevant here—but it is not a long technical exposition

153

that is needed, just an explanation of what the child is wanting from the adults in these kinds of situation, and why. And, as always throughout a playgroup course, the explanation has to be given in the knowledge that the attitudes of those listening vary widely. No one must be made to feel that she has been wrong or silly, or that she may have done real harm to her own children. No one must be so fiercely armed with new knowledge that she rushes home and says to her husband, 'You *are* wrong about not letting John wear my hats at home, Miss X says so.'

Help is needed with the care of the home corner during play. Do we insist that every child is made to restore law and order before leaving, even if it means calling him away from the water tray which may have caught his fancy as he was 'going to work'? Or do we turn a blind eye, and allow the boys to turn it into a robbers' cave, with the dolls thrown outside because 'they're dead Indians we have just shot'? Or do we wait until the corner is empty, and quietly tidy it so that a passing child may be drawn into it because it looks so irresistibly inviting?

Always the queries come back to 'what do you do when . . . ?' And the answers need to be given by someone who understands what can happen when under-fives play together; who understands just why the situations that arise are baffling to the average mother; and who can create the warm and accepting climate of opinion that enables people to modify their own attitudes as they begin to see situations from the child's point of view.

After a practical session on the home corner, which has led to discussion embracing both the children's point of view, the attitude of the mothers present in the playgroup, and suggestions for avoiding and dealing with possible problems, then the students really need to be asked to jot down what is said and done in the home corner for discussion the following week. Again, if all observations are duplicated and read consecutively, then the learning is reinforced.

Painting

Sometimes playgroups find that the children are not enjoying painting as much as everyone thought they would; the caretaker may be put out about the paint on the walls, door handles, surrounds and wash basins; the mothers may be complaining that they thought the children would be doing more than 'bringing home these messes'.

Sessions on painting need to deal with every one of these points.

1. A thoroughly practical session in which the adults concerned can mix powder paint, try tube paint, experiment with various ways of thickening powder paint; try various lengths and thicknesses of brush; try various types, colours, shapes and sizes of paper; compare notes as to ways of attaching paper to the easels; organize alternative methods of painting for those without easels; and compare notes as to methods of drying paintings, according to the many limiting factors in most halls.

At the end of this session many people find that their very real fears and anxieties about 'being no good at painting' were groundless, and they begin to say, 'Do you know, I nearly didn't turn up for this painting session! I was never any good at it at school.'

If the tutor is aware of what she is trying to achieve, then the paint-dabblers become aware of the following points: that if there has been adequate planning, the children's paint can be confined to paper, overalls and ground-covering; that painting is unsatisfying unless the colour slips easily and boldly over the paper; that it is frustrating to be told to clear up just when one is becoming excited and involved (moral—give children adequate warning); that it would be unpopular if someone came along and said, 'What's that?' especially as some of them now realize that many of the children may, unfortunately, be as self-conscious and anxious as they themselves were at first.

2. It is essential to have a session looking knowledgeably at an assembled collection of children's paintings, to see what sort of work they produce naturally. It needs to be explained that children paint much as they cut teeth—it happens, each stage giving way to the next at the appropriate stage of the child's general maturation and experience. Only when adults understand that painting is one of nature's ways of indicating and furthering development and is also a child's means of communication, do they begin to see that teaching or copying have no place at this stage.

155

Since the children's paintings speak for themselves, it is comparatively easy to accept that 'this is what they do at three and four years of age', especially if each student has brought with her a roll of playgroup paintings, and can find examples to match the stages as the tutor shows and explains her examples collected from playgroup children.

Finally, when the practical sessions include fingerpainting, collage and potato prints, it is necessary for the tutor to say at the end, 'Now watch it! You are all dying to rush off and buy six pounds of potatoes; you are all prepared to spend an entire evening cutting them into different shapes—and you can't wait to rush into the playgroup to offer the children *your* pleasure! Do be careful. Many of the children won't yet have had their fill of splodging about in one colour, or discovering that they can produce lines, dots, dashes and islands of colour. Leave them to go naturally through their own stages of discovery, printing will come later as they discover it accidentally and then want to pursue their discovery.'

If the session with dough and the subsequent observations have come before this session, it is easy enough to refer them back to the many examples of children discovering pattern making as they flattened the dough by leaning on it. It really does begin to dawn on people that the children progress naturally through their play, as long as we have made the sort of provision that makes it possible—and as long as we are learning to be so observant that we can spot the moment of real learning, and distinguish it from 'naughtiness' or 'messing about'.

Tutors report the same crop of questions at every session; they are so universal that we learn to have examples of work at hand to illustrate each point. 'What do you do when a child does a lovely picture, and then spoils it by painting all over it? We find we have to stand by the easel to make a dive to rescue their good pictures before they ruin them.' There are so many answers to this one. One playgroup leader said to such a child, 'Oh! Where are your lovely fish?' To which the child sensibly replied, 'Underneath the sea, silly!' Another enquired about the missing house, and was told briefly, 'It's night time.'

Just very occasionally a child will come to a playgroup robbed of all confidence and self-esteem: the parental cry has continually been, 'Don't be silly!' 'Here, let me do it!' 'No!

156

not like that!' 'You can do better than that—look, this way!
No. Try again.' Such a child may be afraid to commit herself
to anything in a playgroup, for fear of reprimand. When eventually she dares to paint it is quite likely that she will choose a
pale colour, and paint minutely in a corner of the paper. If she
sees an adult coming she is likely to scrub her painting out as
if to say, 'I know it's no good, you don't have to tell me, I've
already destroyed it!' It sometimes works for a mother to say,
'What a lovely colour! It's just the colour I should like to have
in my kitchen at home, wouldn't it be lovely to have pinky
curtains like that?' With any luck the child will know the joy
of having produced something worthwhile in adult eyes, and
she may even hand her painting over so that you can 'show the
shop, and then I can see if I can match it'. (But you must keep
your part of the bargain, and bring back the painting and the
patterns to show her.) The child will also have begun to form
a positive relationship, and both verbal and emotional communication will have started.

Usually—and how hard it is for adults to accept this—the
over-brushing is simply a way of saying, 'I've had it! It was
absorbing and fascinating while it lasted, but now I've suddenly
had enough. It's as dead as the dodo and I'm simply crossing
it off.'

In the light of this possible explanation, should we not look
again at our 'take it home to mummy' system? If at 12 o'clock
the children want to do it as a custom, let us then be careful
not to refer to them all as lovely pictures unless we happen to
know that a particular creation gave a particular child a particular satisfaction. New groups might like to consider making
no attempt to start this custom, but to wait and see just how
long it may be before a child says spontaneously, 'Can I take
this home to mummy?' Another common question is 'What do
you do with a mother who receives her offering with "What am
I supposed to do with this then?" or "What, another one of
your messes! Oh well, it can go in the dustbin with the rest!" '
The real answer lies in preventing it from happening.

If no child's name is put down for the playgroup until
mother and child have spent one whole session in the playgroup,
then the playgroup leader can use this one guaranteed occasion
to have an extra helper on duty, so that she is free to sit by the

new mother to explain just what goes on. If the mother begins to understand what a playgroup is all about she will also begin to have some idea of her role, and since one hopes she will have begun to look upon the playgroup leader as a potential friend, she will want to conform to what seems to be expected of mothers on the question of settling-in, sending children in play clothes, and valuing (but not over-valuing) their unaided offerings.

In many areas the playgroup people don't yet know what they don't know, and they just ask for 'a session on painting'. The result is often that a distinctly nervous infant art expert is called in to do the job, with no briefing of any kind: she takes along a folio of the work done by infants (what else *can* she take?) and is careful to say, at intervals, 'Now do remember that my children are two or three years older than yours, so don't expect this sort of standard.'

We must realize that it's not just a case of our little frogs not being able to jump as high, or as far, as the bigger school frogs; we are dealing with tadpoles. They will eventually be frogs, but where their painting is concerned they are still at quite a different stage of development. They paint because they must, it comes spontaneously from within, and it develops slowly as the child develops.

Story-telling

Most mothers are convinced that they could not possibly tell a story, and it is with the utmost surprise that they agree that, yes, they have often told their children stories about things they did when they were little. They need to realize that playgroup story-telling is as relaxed as this; in fact they can tell some of those same true stories to little groups until they gain confidence to tell a 'proper' story. Even though story-telling is the aim, it is still helpful to spend some time on story reading, and half-telling, half-reading from an illustrated book.

Tape recorders can be useful; until we hear ourselves reading a story most of us have no idea how much too quickly we read. Since most mothers read comics and library books aloud at some time or other it is helpful to learn to do it well.

Obvious as it may seem, groups need to practise showing picture books to each other. They truly do not know that you cannot see a cockerel on a gate if a picture is six inches by four and flashed around a semi-circle sitting on the floor six feet away. Even though the ultimate aim is still story-*telling* this exercise is useful, once people discover for themselves how much longer it takes to see something unexpected than to see what you yourself are exhibiting, then the situation can be transposed. They can be helped to be more patient when trying to point out to children objects in the room, on a shelf, in a shop, from a bus or car window.

Once everybody has managed to tell a short personal story to a small group of children, then it helps if a practised story-teller can tell stories to the students; their faces show quite clearly that they are not watching this as a demonstration at all, they are listening to the story for its own sake. Many delighted tutors report, 'It was a joy to watch them, and at the end they all clapped me!' Quite often they will ask for an immediate repeat, and this time the tutor knows that they are both memorizing the story, and absorbing the sight and sound of her telling it. These students learn by imitation very quickly indeed, and will say the following week, 'I told it just as you did, and they sat spellbound—it was one of the most marvellous things that has ever happened to me!'

The next stage is to demonstrate how you can tell a story in such a way that the thread remains unbroken, whilst at the same time indicating clearly just how you cope with one child wanting to go to the lavatory, another rubbing his heels along the floor, another sucking his thumb loudly, and the inevitable one who interrupts because something that you said sparked off his own train of thought.

Time, and more practice, needs to be spent considering the ways of looking at books with children. Particular reference needs to be made to the shy child, or the child who finds speech difficult: the very human reaction is to ask the child a dozen questions, looking at him in anticipation of an answer. It is more helpful to keep our eyes on the book, and to ask questions so vaguely that there is no need for an answer. 'A cat! Have you got one of these at home? We have, a big black one . . .' and over goes the page. If our voices are low enough, and warmly soothing, there usually comes a moment when the child will comment, even if only a single word, 'Dog!' and it takes all our self-control not to say, 'There! You have got a tongue in your head after all!' Students burst out laughing here—for every single one of them has already fallen into that trap. Where there is laughter there is learning.

Books need time to themselves. What sort of books, what size, weight, type of illustrations? How to display them? How to care for them? Where to get them?

Interest corners

Few playgroups can leave anything out in the playroom after the session, and few playgroup leaders can carry a complete interest corner to a playgroup—neither should they, for the finding and bringing are part of the joy.

It is interesting to put the students in the children's situation, and more revealing than they expected. It sounds simple enough to ask them all to bring a bottle of some sort the following week so that they can form a collection for everyone to see. It is when they arrive that they become as children. One will take a baby's bottle from her holdall, whilst another will bring out a beer bottle, each looking at the other in momentary horror, each certain she has done the wrong thing. There will probably be medicine bottles, aspirin bottles, wine bottles, shampoo bottles, squash bottles. Together they comprise a wide variety of shapes, colours, sizes and materials. And suddenly the students see beauty in the commonplace, and begin to see the world as children see it with their fresh eyes.

Collections can be made of objects all of a given colour; of objects to feel; collections of vegetables, leaves, brushes, wooden objects. Playgroup leaders need to be aware of the need to take one or two things themselves to their playgroups, in order to alleviate the disaster that could befall the child who forgets, or did not know about the plan. Practice is needed in arranging the objects so that their beauty is enhanced; and in learning how to talk about the objects naturally and easily so that it does not become a question-and-answer session, guaranteed to kill the emotional response. Intellectual and emotional growth need to be encouraged together, not at the expense of each other.

Music

As a playgroup adviser so aptly put it, 'We have years and years of punitive music teaching to undo with these mums.' Most of them find singing in front of each other even more of an ordeal than telling stories, and much the same methods need to be used in order to restore confidence.

Nursery rhymes are part of our heritage, and should be passed on in the same way that they came to us—by singing and chanting in intimate groups. It doesn't matter if we 'can't sing', near talking will do as long as the rhythm is there and words come over clearly.

Jingles and fingerplays are another simple delight, and few playgroups know enough of them. Many courses are getting into the habit of learning one or two new ones at the beginning of each session, and repeating those of the week before, to make certain that the learning has been retained. It helps if the words are written down, and loose-leaf files can be compiled of story outlines, rhymes and fingerplays.

There is a delightful videotape, made in Bath, showing a child apparently paying no attention to a singing group; her back is turned as she plays with a table toy, and suddenly the camera picks up her face, to show that her lips are moving soundlessly as she absorbs what is going on without appearing to do so. Similarly, children actively involved in the group may only be at the stage of forming the words soundlessly, or of singing them aloud but out of tune. It takes some children a long while before their voices will produce the sound that their minds tell them they are trying to make.

From this small beginning people become more confident and go on to rhythms, using hands and feet to accompany songs, or music played on a piano, a recorder, a drum, or a record player.

Another source of music, so simple that it is constantly overlooked, is the provision of familiar objects that produce sounds; a collection of bells ranging through jingle bells, Swiss cow bells, various small hand bells, to school-type bells. Jars or bottles of water filled to different levels give a simple scale, and a tone that changes as the different strikers are available. Chime bars, bicycle bells and hooters, sealed tins with different contents, a triangle, Indian bells or a more expensive item from a range of real musical instruments all offer experience of sounds, some of which are beautiful. All these enable the

161

children to make their own personal discoveries through experiment. But it is unlikely that they will have the opportunity if the adults in the group have not first had their own enthusiasm roused by personal experiment.

Movement to music is often more difficult to tackle. A group needs to be very relaxed and stable before children feel able to move spontaneously with the music as it carries them along. There have been several occasions when I have seen children put on their own records, or ask to have one put on for them, and then dance with grace and dreamy concentration, quite oblivious to anything or anyone else. Some tutors are able to carry students along with them as they themselves move to music, and when it happens everyone is exhilarated and can hardly believe that it was really they who kicked off their shoes, jettisoned their handbag, and let go. Care is needed if we are to build up confidence, but try to encourage students to foster free movement to music rather than resort to the familiar pattern of 'Let's be giants . . . fairies . . . soldiers'.

Notes need to be kept of suitable records, some strong in rhythm, some strong in mood. Practice is needed in finding the right place on an LP, and discussion as to how long an excerpt children can absorb, and how often it needs to be played. Discussion is needed on how, when and where any of these musical activities shall take place, with particular reference to problems of space and noise.

Finally the moment arrives when the question of percussion bands is brought to light. For many people music and percussion bands are synonymous and two methods of using percussion instruments are very widespread indeed.

1. They are used as sound-effects to accompany nursery rhymes or are freely available at all times. 'Music' can then be delightfully relaxed and rhythmical, as jingle bells shake, scrapers scrape and drums beat out a real rhythm. It can be particularly happy when the children prance round to 'Jingle Bells'; and even more joyous when a child thoughtfully picks up an instrument to try it out attentively, to be joined by other interested children, at which point an adult may quietly put on a record or sit down at the piano, and slowly the majority (or even all) of the children join in and an impromptu

162

McNamara's Band wends its way spontaneously round the room.

It is much less happy when all the children are sat down in a circle and rehearsed; again and again poor William misses his cue on the cymbal as the clock strikes 'One' and again and again everybody goes back to the beginning until it is right. There is no longer joy in music, only a growing tension and a desire to please.

2. All the instruments (of which the majority are tin drums) are kept in a cupboard or box, and at a given point in the morning there is 'music', and the invariable system is that as the children march past the cupboards or the box they are given (or occasionally select) an instrument. As soon as they have it they are free to make as much noise as they like. The noise level can positively hurt, and the helpers put their hands over their ears to shut it out—so do some of the non-participating children—but they willingly endure it under the mistaken impression that it is what children like and need. Indeed it is not. Sound and noise are not synonymous and we hope to encourage children to listen, distinguish, discriminate, respond and to enjoy.

Written and shared observations on children's responses to sounds and music are revealing, and students become more aware of what it is that they are trying to quicken in children. A child once said of a lullaby, 'That's pink music, play it again.' Another child said of a recorded march played by a brass band, 'It's fat music, let's have some more, I like it.'

Room layout

It is common to find a large slide in the middle of a small hall; the children swish down and often run on to the end wall, or they scramble up and dash round (some to the right, some to the left) for another turn, and the result is that a floor space quite disproportionate to the size of the hall is monopolized by this one activity. If it is moved to the end of the hall, set up parallel to the wall and about two feet away from it, then all the children can be encouraged to go between the slide and the wall on their way for another turn, and much less floor space is needed.

Discussion is needed about how best to use the unwanted

163

fixtures that exist in so many halls—billiard tables, stacks of chairs, protruding coke stoves. Discussion is needed as to the placing of sand and water: together or apart? How much space is needed for painting? How much for a home corner? Where will noisy activities be least disturbing? How does one balance the value of table-top space against floor space?

Students need to rearrange a room in several ways before they are able to go back to their own playgroup and re-plan it to its best advantage.

How are systems of law and order to be operated over small equipment? How many puzzles need to be out at any one time? What, if anything, does an adult do about a table covered with the jumbled pieces of four or five puzzles? What arrangements can be made for the dressing-up clothes? Is it possible to provide a mirror? How can clearing away be organized in such a way that the children help, even if they are unable to carry things down into the cellar or up into the attic?

Where could stories be told? What can the children sit on? How can we avoid trailing across the room to fetch chairs or mats every time a story or singing group forms spontaneously? If the room is small which things will need to be put away, or not used, during story and music? Where can paintings be dried? Where can the children find enough space to be able to learn to put on their own shoes and coat? How much space does a child need for this extraordinarily complicated task? Where are parents going to sit for elevenses? How, when and where are the children going to have elevenses?

There is no substitute for the reality. We all learn by doing, and the more senses that are involved in the doing, the greater the reinforcement.

UNDERSTANDING CHILDREN

This section makes no claim to offer right suggestions and solutions. It is an attempt to introduce new tutors to the needs of students in this field of playgroup relationships. Eight years of tutoring and contact with tutors and students have confirmed my belief that all the human problems, needs, misunderstandings and enthusiasms of one geographical area are common to all others.

'Difficult' children

Playgroup people ask for psychology quite regularly, especially on a first course; it seems to be one of the first subjects that automatically comes to mind. By trial and error over the country we learn that what they really mean by this request is 'Please can we have someone to tell us what to do with difficult children?'

Many psychologists, especially those attached to child guidance clinics, are pronounced 'Wonderful!' But sometimes they have not understood quite what playgroup people need. One such discovered the genuine needs for himself when he started a playgroup with his wife, in the hope that when it was running smoothly with a small group of normal children, he would be able to introduce several of his special need children from the clinic. Long before there was any thought of introducing the clinic children, he tells ruefully how he had to telephone the local nursery school head to ask if she would go and speak to them all as 'I know precisely why each child is behaving as he is, but we don't seem to know what to do about it!'

Possibly the first need is to explain the difference between a child with difficulties and a child whose behaviour in the group causes difficulty to the adults concerned. The latter may be blissfully normal, whilst the adults may be unduly anxious and insecure. It takes time to get rid of the idea that either children or adults are to blame. The difficulties that need to be discussed are usually these.

The shy child. He or she is sometimes confused with the anxious child. Many mothers feel that all children should be outgoing, and if their child is rather shy they feel that it is a reflection on their upbringing.

Reassurance is needed here: some perfectly normal children are shy. If a child is anxious and unable to join in anything, then the adults need to be helped to understand the situation from the child's point of view. The usual overture of an adult anxious to help is to go up to the child and say, 'Would you like to play with the sand? No? Then what about the water? Or would you like to come and see our books?' They have not understood that the child is unable to make a decision of any kind at this stage of such a new experience.

165

Help is needed in suggesting that such a child might feel safe sitting in a stout wooden chair, with her back to the wall, with a friendly adult near, while she just watches. After all, it must be as enthralling as a first visit to the theatre! All one wants to do is to watch. Many of us can remember what it felt like to be a wallflower at a dance, and can recall how welcome it would have been if occasionally (before we became frozen into immobility) someone had sat beside us to talk, or if a passing person had said, casually, 'Come and listen to the band!' or 'I'm going to have something to eat—come and join me!' or 'Here, catch!' as a balloon was tossed into our laps. Sometimes an easel can be moved invitingly near; or a dumpling of dough can be put into nervous hands; or a table with a simple toy or puzzle can be put close beside (but not as a prison bar in front of) the child.

People need to share their experiences of such children in playgroups; someone is bound to say, 'Don't worry! We had a child like that and then, suddenly, after two or six or ten weeks she was up and away!' But help is needed in suggesting that a child who sits under a table with tightly closed eyes for weeks on end needs expert help. At least some guideline between the normal and the abnormal or sub-normal should be indicated.

The bossy child. The description is usually, 'You honestly can't call her naughty or aggressive—but it's jolly difficult to have someone who is everlastingly saying, "I'll do it! You can't do it! No, not like that! I must have the drum, you can have the shakers. I'll be the mother and you've got to be auntie!"'

Sometimes a playgroup leader will say, 'We've given up having our percussion instruments altogether, we just couldn't cope with the everlasting squabbles.' Endless help is needed in indicating the difference between those episodes that can best be left for the children to resolve themselves whilst the adults turn a blind eye, and those episodes where it is right and proper for the adult to say brightly but firmly, 'No, it's time for Jim to have a turn today. Would you like the triangle or the bells?'

The child who takes things. There is a difference here in motives. With some children it is a straightforward temptation; the new Dinky fire engine that Robert brought to show everybody is irresistible! But for some children the object is of no intrinsic

166

value at all; they take because they feel empty in some way that they don't understand. Pockets may bulge with odd pieces of jigsaw puzzles, a bead, a grubby hair ribbon, a thrown-away paper hankie, a nail or two, a painting folded up into a thick wad, or a farm animal. Or it may be a single small object each day. The inner cry is 'I want! I need!' and the real answer is almost always love and attention.

But what are playleaders to do about the taking? If the child gets away with it several things can happen. The mother may discover the things when she gets home, and may create a real scene in her anxiety that she has a child who is a thief. Or she may be so casual that she does not bother to return the precious missing piece of the jigsaw puzzle; it is easier just to throw it away with the rest of the rubbish. Neither reaction is going to help the child. The child may feel guilty as people complain about the missing piece of puzzle, and be quite unable to own up in case he loses yet more of he-knows-not-what. So he keeps quiet and his conscience is a burden. This does not help either.

The playgroup leader may discover the hidden treasure and offer a little homily on 'You wouldn't like it if I came to your house and took some of your things, would you?' At three or four a child cannot really grasp the idea of the playgroup leader walking into his house and actually removing something. So he listens to the reproving tone of voice (which he can understand) and shuts out the implication (which he can't understand) and the net result is a feeling of being even more 'minus' than he was before.

Example helps more than anything else. If the playgroup leader has a few bits and pieces in her overall pocket (and which of us doesn't collect the odd things here and there during the morning?) she can produce them and say, 'Look what I've found! Has anyone else been kind enough to pick things up from the floor to keep them safe?' At this invitation to praise the small magpie is usually the first to offer his hoard. He can be thanked, and invited to help the playgroup leader to put all the odds and ends in the right boxes. Not only is his conscience clear, he is also being singled out for the loving and appreciative attention that he craved in the first place.

Invariably the adults say, 'But isn't that just encouraging other children to take things?' Why should they, if they do not need this special attention? Children are far more perceptive than most of us, they seem to know that such a child has a special need, and they expect us to offer help where it is needed. If the singling-out is done naturally and easily only the child himself will know just how much your warmth means to him, for only he is not able to take it for granted.

The untruthful child. The telling of 'lies' is usually very distressing for mothers. Playgroup leaders can be every bit as worried as 'just mothers', especially if they have had a nursery or teacher training, for then they feel additionally guilty that it should happen to them. There is a real fear that the child might grow up to be delinquent, that lies might lead to stealing or even worse—that their child might be one of those whose dire doings are reported in the press, and of whom it is said in court that they 'have no moral sense'.

Because the lie, or rather untruth, itself is so disturbing, people tend not to be able to look it quietly in the face and examine possible motives. There are several explanations:

1. We may underrate the effect of our 'cross voice'. How many of us withdraw, or lash out, if our husbands have cause to use a cross voice to us? If a cross voice is habitual, then children learn to shut it out; but if it is reasonably rare, then it conveys a wealth of meaning—and a sensitive child may try to avoid such a tirade. As one child said after being reduced to tears, 'Mummy, why did you think I would know that? I haven't been in the world before.'

2. For some children a lie is the equivalent of putting a toe into the sea to test the temperature. 'John has broken the teapot' may indicate that the child is waiting for the reaction. If it is 'Oh no! He's a naughty boy, and I'll give him a good hiding when I catch him' then one small candidate for a hiding may slide off out of reach. If it is, 'Well, we'd better get a dustpan and brush, hadn't we?' then a relieved helper may tag along behind saying, 'I was trying to fill up the vase like you do, and the lid fell off.'

3. Some children find it truly difficult to distinguish between fact and fantasy, they can move so easily between the two in

their play. Some children have vivid imaginations; some indulge in wishful thinking, and 'We have fish fingers and beans for tea every day' means 'I wish that we could.'

The sharing of playgroup experiences is valuable and as the universality of examples is recognized so anxiety lessens and home examples come in profusion. This lessening of tension and deepening of understanding paves the way both in playgroups and homes for relationships that do not aggravate this natural phase of development.

The aggressive child. If the tutor says 'You know the one I mean, the one—usually a boy—who makes you fly to the register to find out how soon he'll be five!' there is the usual burst of relieved laughter. Incredibly nearly every playgroup leader thinks that it is just her bad luck to be landed with such a child. So first his universality needs to be recognized, and any false hopes dispelled as we assure them that our dear friend William is a permanent part of the playgroup scene. He must be accepted. Then we must deal with the question 'Why does this child's aggression worry me so?' There are usually several different answers to this.

'It's so unfair! After all we've done to raise the money for the equipment and to get the thing started, this one child spoils it all'; 'I get all hot and bothered. Suppose it spreads? If all the children got out of control like this there could be a real riot, and I wouldn't be able to control it'; or 'It makes me mad, because he's spoiling it for the others'; or 'I feel guilty, because I just can't like this child and I know I should'. Once all these very human reactions are out in the open they can be discussed. Only when people are reassured and feel less fearful and antagonistic are they free to consider the child's point of view.

Next, we must face the fact that most playgroup leaders would love to be able to wave a wand to take away the aggression 'because he'd be a really nice child without it'. It simply has not dawned on most people that if we could take away all the aggression, then we would be left with a child who was unable to attack work, or problems, or life itself. This is usually an eye-opener, and people are prepared to say, 'Well, all right—but he still can't rush round attacking the smaller children'. So now the problem becomes 'How do we channel the aggression so that it is socially acceptable?'

Since Williams tend to love bashing, some time needs to be spent in discussing what can legitimately be bashed. Fists can bash into both clay and dough; one William attacked a lump of dough viciously, saying through clenched teeth, 'I'll nip you and pinch you till you bleed!' Eventually the frantic figure relaxed, and manipulating the dough became a deeply satisfying and soothing experience. A hammer and nails can be a splendid outlet—but before the tutor gets as far as '. . . and nails' there is an outcry of 'Oh no!' and 'You simply don't know what our particular William is like, he'd wreck the joint . . . and kill a child or two!' Clearly it is no use making noises about 'In all my thirty years not once has a child . . . etc., etc.' The panic-reaction has to be taken seriously, and carpentry may have to be introduced as one little log of wood, standing meekly in a plastic washing-up bowl (so that the dance floor isn't scratched), with a pound of one- and two-inch nails lurking at the bottom of a golden syrup tin, and one nice workman-like tack hammer. Step by step one has to go through the preliminary processes by which one has previously caught William in the act of bashing Horace, and has said to him, 'No you can't bash Horace—but I'll tell you what you could bash.'

Williams love to tear and stamp and smash. And there is no reason why they shouldn't when cardboard boxes and cartons are so easy to come by. But there will come a time when you need to say in advance, 'William, I can't get any more boxes for tomorrow, so if you want any for then you had better keep one or two safely.' Or bigger and better cases could be found from a shop selling televisions and washing machines, and these may then lead to creative games rather than destruction.

Contrary to most people's doubts, Williams are usually excellent water carriers and if they have carefully carried four half-buckets of water from the kitchen to the water tray (with a helpful adult at each end of the journey) they are usually the first to complain if someone makes a mess—it is a sort of 'after all I've done for you!' reaction. And they can become custodians of the pail and mopping-up cloth.

The discussion about everybody's William can go on interminably, and tutors have their work cut out to see to it that it does not degenerate into a moaning session. The need is for the adults to put themselves into William's woolly jumper, and to view the world from there. Once again, mother-involvement is highly relevant. There is more than a hint of moral judgment on Williams' mothers, and sentences tend to begin 'She's the sort of woman who . . .'. Playgroup leaders will even say, 'I've told her that if William doesn't behave I shall have to think seriously about keeping him.' Alas, it is even harder to put ourselves in William's mother's woolly jumper. Why is it so much easier to be negative than positive? Why don't we wait until William does just one thing right (even if it was an accident that he happened to open the door when we were standing near enough to say, 'Thank you! I was wondering how I was going to open the door with all these things to carry. Could you shut it behind me?') and then we could say to William's mother at twelve o'clock, 'William has been most helpful this morning, haven't you, William?' Most mothers know their reactions if a staff member at school even hints at less than perfect work or behaviour from their offspring; yet knowing how they bristle, they will do exactly the same thing to a playgroup mother!

Another difficulty lies in coping with William when his mother is in the playgroup. Let us all admit, fair and square, that some playgroup leaders feel that they simply cannot cope with this sort of situation at all. It is no disgrace to anyone: it is a simple fact, and must be accepted as simply as William's existence must be accepted. But let us not overlook the fact that many playgroup leaders can, and do, cope with this superbly. And by doing so in front of the mother they are often able to offer her quite a new approach to this same situation at home. In short, it is the mothers of Williams who so badly need to be in a well-run playgroup—but they are the ones who will not risk being there if they feel they are going to be blamed, or got at. It takes generosity of heart, tact and maturity for a playgroup leader to be as prepared to accept William's mother as naturally as she accepts him.

Real psychology belongs to courses far in advance of any-thing that most playgroup people need. Sometimes they want it on a course, but if they haven't any real understanding of these very human difficulties it may be very much worse than nothing—for there is the temptation to deal psychologically with problems that simply do not exist. As one mother said, 'I don't know! A few years ago we just called a child naughty, and now we say to each other earnestly that we suspect a minor degree of maladjustment.' The use of jargon can blind us to our own insensitivity in meeting human situations.

Child development

The presentation of this subject is all-important. No sooner does some expert come along to talk about it than there is universal dismay. The criticism is always the same, 'The last thing in the world that we want is to be told about babies waving arms and legs in their prams! We've "had" that stage, we know every single bit of it, and we've lived through it day and night with two or three or four children—so we know the individual variations as well.' The expert explains that one must begin at the beginning, for every stage is dependent on the one that went before; they hazard an accurate guess that even though the mothers may have noticed that certain stages come and go, they have probably not understood why. It is of no avail. The psychological rejection of systematic child development in an early course is almost universal; unreasonable it may be but mothers tend to be highly allergic to whole sessions spent on a stage that they want to forget as quickly as possible. The exhaustion associated with it is too recent and so, too, is the anxiety associated with dread of another unwanted pregnancy which still haunts many mothers.

In those situations where some people are interested at this stage there are unexpected pitfalls. One group of playgroup people said that they 'had got as far as the nervous system', but there had been no reference to the fact that it is better not to hand scissors to a child at this stage of development, because we are almost bound to offer them to his right hand, he is almost bound to accept them, and may struggle to use them, and if he is unsuccessful it may be due to the fact that at this stage of development he may not yet have established the fact that he is predominantly left-handed. As has been said many times before, it is down to earth practical knowledge, reinforced by playgroup examples, that playgroup people need.

The practical application of child development should weave through the course as a single unbroken thread.

It is useless to read little moral lectures to Williams, because at this stage of their development children are simply not able to extract any meaning from so many words expressing a morality that they cannot yet understand. This becomes clear to playgroup people when they are asked if anyone ever said to their husband in the evening, 'Honestly, he doesn't take a blind bit of notice. I was patient, and reasonable, and I explained it perfectly clearly—and he did the same thing again the minute my back was turned!' This goes home!

So, too, does 'If you want Horace to have the pleasure of giving his mother an invitation, or a message, and he is going home with a neighbour, don't expect him to learn it by heart. He may know it perfectly, but by the time he has had a chat about a red bus, and a dog, and the butcher's van on the way home he will have forgotten it. Either ask the neighbour to remind him at the garden gate, or write a note and slip it in the palm of his glove—he'll forget to look in his pocket, but the chances are that it will fall to the floor when he removes his glove, and he can know his moment of satisfaction as he re-members to deliver his important message.' It takes endless practical suggestions and explanations before many adults really begin to become aware of the very real limitations of being three or four years old.

Observations

Here most of us have to re-think, and try out various methods. It becomes clear very early on in the course that parents tend to see what they look for, and familiarity with their own child has led, in self-defence, to the situation where their minds, eyes, and ears, only half notice. The maternal warning system flashes, 'He's quiet, what's he up to?', and the only answer she needs is the quick reassurance of a glance that conveys 'All's well, he's not doing any harm', and back she goes to her tasks. This quality of looking and listening carries over into the playgroup, and it is quite difficult to alter such a deeply ingrained habit.

The usual methods of trial and error are these.

1. It is suggested that everyone chooses a single child, and watches him throughout one session. The first attempt may be, 'He played with sand, then water, then had a swing...'. Later

attempts may enlarge upon this and one may read, 'He spent a long time just tipping sand out of a spoon, then he . . .' .

Slowly the ability to watch more carefully is fostered, and if the same child is watched throughout the term a student is surprised to find that she has a living picture of a child developing.

2. It is further suggested that everyone chooses one activity to watch. This they tend to find more difficult, for it often involves watching several children at once round, say, the sand tray. Their powers of observation are not usually equal to the tasks of 'seeing' several children simultaneously.

3. Sometimes charts are issued with detailed points for observation set out. This is the least happy solution of all, for what with balancing the chart on their laps, and timing the activities with a wrist watch, and noting conversations and moods, the task becomes an effort of co-ordination and concentration to the point where it becomes impossible to enter into the spirit of the play.

4. An experimental situation may be outlined to the whole class, and they may be asked to set it up in their playgroup the following week. For example, it may be suggested that a plastic bowl containing about an inch of water, two adult floor scrubbing brushes and two large cakes of soap be put upon a wooden table or bench or floor. The students can be asked to lurk in the backgound and jot down what they see and hear.

The following week everybody is amazed that the children found it absorbing. Greater revelation is to come. If all the jottings are duplicated and clipped together as primitive books, with a copy for everyone, then child development unfolds before their eyes as they read of different children repeating the same stages of discovery. Not only this, but they begin to notice themselves in relation to the children. For example, most children discover that the large wet cake of soap slips out of their grasp repeatedly, and invariably the exclamation is 'Naughty soap!'—and slowly it dawns on everyone that naughty means 'it won't do what I want it to do, when I want it done'. This definition of naughty is a complete surprise to many of them.

Another aspect of play to come through is the ebb and flow of the emotional tide. For example, two children scrubbed to the peak of their enjoyment, commenting at intervals, 'Aren't we hard-working ladies?' and, 'We're not playing today, we're working.' At the peak of enjoyment the older one said to the provider of this blissful experience, 'I'll do everything you tell me to do for ever and ever!' And the younger one echoed, 'So will I!' And then the downward trend started with 'That's my soap . . . you're scrubbing my bit . . . you hit my hand', ending with the younger one throwing down her brush with the cry, 'I shan't play any more!' Suddenly it registers that at the height of their enjoyment the children clearly felt that they were working, and only when the enjoyment lessened was the word play used—and there is insight into the nature of play from the child's point of view.

Slowly, very slowly, they begin to understand children, play and themselves.

LANGUAGE AND COMMUNICATION

People on courses tend to confuse the words language, speech and communication. Tutors could spend more time on this, and it is helpful to begin by discussing communication. We have all known what it is to communicate without words at all. Conversely, we have all had the frustrating experience of explaining something most carefully in words, only to be completely misunderstood. Again, we have all been deeply moved by written or spoken words that we did not really understand. Children communicate with their parents long before they learn to speak. At the playgroup stage, communication is still more compelling than words for children. Our words can say clearly, 'No, we don't throw sand', but a child knows at once by our tone, our stance, our expression if 'No' means 'I hope you won't, for if you do I'm not sure that I shall know what to do about it.' We have communicated the very opposite of the message that we gave him in words. The child is likely to act upon the communication without reference to the words, and the sand is thrown.

Adults in a playgroup (or indeed a home) need to 'communicate' warmth, approval, interest, kindness, justice, humour, tolerance, and the sort of security whereby everyone knows how

175

far they can go before the line is firmly drawn. Then, within this framework of communication (partly a matter of tone, touch, expression, concern, muscular tension, pace) language is introduced to deepen communication and widen knowledge. No matter how gifted we may be in the use of language, its impact is enhanced or diminished by the quality of the communication between speaker and listener.

What of children who come to playgroups at the age of, say, four-and-a-half, with the linguistic ability of a one-year-old? Do we say to ourselves, 'Heavens! School in six months, we'd better concentrate on him like mad?' It all depends on what we mean by 'concentrate'. Better to forget the word and substitute 'communicate'.

But if he has not known the warm bond of expressive love between mother and child that fosters communication, then his ability to make a relationship with other people, or allow them to make one with him, may be as impoverished as his language.

Progress is likely to be slow at first, since he has neither language nor emotion to offer, and little capacity to receive either. In this sort of situation we have to make the first move, but this does not mean that we have to advance upon him with a dozen questions: 'Would you like to play with the sand? No? Well, would you like to see our goldfish? Or our kitchen? My word, you are a smart little boy, shall we hang that lovely coat on a dear little hook with your picture on it?' Such a child's language barrier is like an adult's who goes into a French shop and says a carefully rehearsed little bit about '*du pain, s'il vous plait*', only to be drowned in a torrent of French. We might black out completely so that we could not even recognize the odd words that we did know, and that they *must* have used. If only they had had the understanding to smile, raise an appreciative eyebrow, and throw us an encouraging '*C'est bien!*', then we could have smiled and opened a purse, and said with growing comprehension '*Combien?*' If the answer was beyond comprehension, the 'communication' by that time might have made it possible laughingly to hold out a palm full of assorted small coins.

Are children, who are foreigners to so much adult language, so very different? Once adults begin to identify with such a child, then they can see the need to speak slowly and quietly, with a bare minimum of words at first; to keep in contact with him by a smile or wave across the room, so that he never feels isolated, even if he chooses to be physically isolated for a period of watching. We need to remind ourselves that he may not yet have heard a dozen words in a day; how could he possibly understand a dozen in a single sentence?

A student once said, 'Yes, I can see all that, but you haven't told us *what* to say', and this request must be taken seriously. The realization that children can know so little comes as a shock to many. We need to be able to offer simple advice, such as 'If you are offered a sloshy painting it will be more helpful to say "A *red* one!" than "Lovely!" ' Or 'Fill out your words with gestures: if you pat the chair beside you and smile a welcome, the words "Come here and sit by me" will register accurately.'

The next stage is helping adults to know when to speak and when to be silent. New learning starts with 'doing'. This period of exploration is usually silent, for children are like sponges, absorbing with their eyes, ears, noses, skin surface and muscles (mouths, too, quite often) vivid sensations to which our own senses are often blunted. All this learning they need to do in their own way, and in their own time. They may grunt if surprised by weight, hardness, wetness, or laugh aloud at the unexpected outcome of an action, but these are involuntary noises. They will be living wholly in the immediate experience. We have no right to break into these deeply private moments of discovery. It is when the 'doing' is over that they need us to be there, so that they can tell us what happened: later they will be able to forecast events—'I'm going to fill it up to the top!' and we can then further both knowledge and vocabulary if we say 'Is it heavy? Heavier than the pink one? As heavy as the bottle?'

Eventually someone in the class will say, 'What about speech?' and she will usually mean 'What do we do about teaching the children to speak nicely?' or 'What would you do with children who use rude words?' or else it may be 'What do you do about a child whose mother says in his hearing "We can't get a word out of him, I don't think he's got a tongue in his head"?'

All these things need to be discussed, but they fall into place

177

once people have begun to understand the importance of communication. Finally tutors need to establish the link between the children in the playgroup and their mothers. At the end of the morning some children rush up to their mothers full of news, some suddenly 'go quiet' and need to be taken home and fed before their energy returns, and some mothers and children need the mediation of another person. Communication between some parents and children is so poor that it needs either to be introduced or re-established. The playgroup leader needs, from her observation and participation, to be able to accompany the child to his mother, saying something like, 'Do you know what happened when Peter pushed a big empty bottle under the water this morning?' If Peter wants and is able to reply to the effect that 'It made gobble-gobble noises and bubbles came out of it' several things of importance will have happened. Peter will have laid hold of the knowledge that empty bottles and water behave in a certain way; this lays the foundations of much later knowledge relating to air displacement, volume, weight, etc. And Peter's mother may sense (even if she does not understand) that the playgroup leader feels that this happening was something of value. Peter feels himself to be the focal point of both these important adults in his life, who are united in approval of him. Peter and his mother may seek to repeat this brief period of satisfying communication.

The essence of a playgroup course is this extra dimension of parent involvement. We must constantly be aware of the gaps that exist between what children know, what the students think children know, and what we think the students know about children. *We all assume too much.* Many reminiscences and observations have to be shared before common ground is established and we can learn together to meet children's needs. There are many people on courses who, given additional insights on the mother/child relationship, have a great deal to offer to parents as well as to children. We need tutors to harness this extra help where it is available.

OTHER NEEDS TO BE MET

These topics are no less important than those explained more fully, but these should be self explanatory.

Settling in new children. This procedure is so important for both parents and children that PPA has produced a publication with this title.

Preparing mothers for rota duty. There is no one infallible way, and the only certainty is that mothers need to be prepared and settled in as carefully as the children. See PPA's 'You Too Can Be a Mother-Helper'.

The choosing of equipment, the basic minimum needed to start a playgroup, the imaginary spending of £100, improvisation, etc.

The mending and making of equipment, dressing-up clothes, etc.

Outdoor play.

Making and using puppets.

Woodwork.

First aid (see PPA publication).

The business and legal side of playgroups (see PPA publication).

Nature, the response to living things.

The special needs of handicapped children.

The role of the playgroup leader.

The relationship between playgroup adults in the playgroup and in the community.

'ADVANCED' COURSES

These are really to give a deepening understanding of all that has gone before, backed every inch of the way by personal observations which indicate that the students truly do have a growing grasp of how children learn to think, and an under-standing of mother/child and adult/adult relationships that enables them to modify their attitudes and begin to live what they have learned.

Tutors cannot rely on written observations to assess the growing ability of the students not only to understand, but to apply what they have understood in the playgroup itself.

It is essential for the students to be able to work in playgroups and for them to be visited by the tutor; first in order that they shall have the stimulation and support of on-the-spot comment; and secondly in order that the tutors shall be able to assess if their courses are really relevant to the needs of each playgroup in its own community. [1]

[1] At a conference for playgroup tutors at Keele University in July 1976 it was felt that a fieldwork course might be the next step after the foundation.

Chapter 13

Playgroup advisers

There is so much that needs to be done in the playgroup movement that calls out for the appointment of playgroup advisers who will take upon themselves the responsibility for initiating playgroups, advising and supporting those already established, devising courses to fit local needs, creating a peripatetic tutoring-team, and harnessing the willing help of voluntary organizations.

By 1973 over a hundred local playgroup advisers had been appointed, mostly infant and nursery advisers who were given time to attend to the needs of playgroups as well. But some were playgroup-only appointments, most part time, made directly by the Education or Social Services committees; others were appointed by local branches or county associations of PPA with money granted by either the Education or Social Services committees; at least one appointment was made possible by a grant from a local charity to the local PPA organization, and another was made by the church at diocesan level.

The professional background of the present advisers is wide and varied, but there are certain qualities that are called for which transcend the original training. Playgroup advisers need to know:

what under-fives need for a full development
what help local parents need in order to embark on a play-group
how help can best be given to stimulate self help
how to balance the needs of the children and the parents so that neither is sacrificed to the other
how to bring in help if necessary, so that the children benefit without the parents feeling belittled
how to ferret out, and use, local talent

180

how to gear help so it doesn't cut across cultural roots, but enables people to grow in understanding and ability in *their* time and way.

Above all, perhaps, they need a balance of realism and idealism which enables them to draw the best out of the parents without expecting the impossible, whilst keeping a constant eye on the quality of play for the children.

WHAT NEEDS TO BE DONE?

1. *The initiating of playgroups*
The most needed playgroups have to be unobtrusively encouraged into being—to enthuse a group into existence can be unwise. The parents themselves have to come to the point of feeling the need for a playgroup; but it takes patience, skill and even a certain wiliness for someone to act as the catalyst.

2. *The starting of playgroups*
Once the decision is taken to apply for registration, help is needed between this point and the opening of the playgroup. In some areas two or three meetings with all the parents involved may be enough to satisfy the adviser that everyone knows what they are about, especially if they have visited nursery schools and other playgroups, and are able to attend a good local playgroup course.

But the more urgently an area needs a playgroup, the more personal help is needed. Experience has shown that the supportive presence of someone is needed at almost every meeting in the early days. And, ideally, someone needs to work with the group in the designated playgroup hall once they reach the stage of planning what to make or buy or improvise: the senses of sight and touch need to reinforce the discussion of what the children will need, and where it will go, how it will be put out, and how it can be managed.

Once the group is started support must continue for at least a year, and 'continue' is the operative word: even after that, the playgroup still needs the support of a well-known and liked person. Neither advisers nor tutors have the time to keep these links intact, and the major part of this befriending over the country is undertaken by PPA's voluntary area organizers.

181

3. *The visiting of playgroups*

The degree of parental involvement and the quality of play can wax and wane, and help needs to be available according to the current position. Sometimes the group is aware of the fact that it needs help and will ask for it; sometimes playgroup leaders have drifted into staleness and are unaware of the fact, and it takes a spontaneous visit for the adviser to be aware of what is happening. One glance at the uninviting junk table may be enough to cause her to drop in a few days later with a collection of coloured scraps of material, feathers, silver paper, corks and walnut shells that she 'thought might be useful'.

One such visit resulted in a rush for the junk table, and a blissfully happy period of activity culminating in a child surveying a haphazard, well-stuck, colourful conglomeration of objects saying, 'Isn't it lovely, I feel like eating it!'

4. *The devising of courses*

The word devising is used advisedly, for no two areas are alike, no two tutors are alike, no two playgroup leaders are alike, and no two premises are alike. The varied needs of playgroup people have been outlined in this report, but only the adviser on the spot can know how best to use her resources in order to go about serving the children and their particular parents.

5. *The setting of standards*

The standard that is wanted lies in the adviser's attitude to people, authorities and playgroups; it is a personal standard of thought, communication and action that springs from a sensitive awareness of people and playgroups *as they are*, combined with the awareness of where they could be, given help and encouragement that stops well short of strain and anxiety.

What is not wanted is a rigid yardstick marked 'standard' against which every playgroup and playgroup leader is measured, with the result that those who most need approval to enable them to grow feel themselves to be judged and found wanting.

SHARING THE LOAD

No one man or woman can do all that is needed. The first PPA adviser to be appointed in ILEA in 1964 started with only eight playgroups; she worked so closely with this small group that when the numbers grew she was able to call upon some of the original people to help her to widen her tutoring force. At least one of the recent advisers found herself with immediate responsibility for 400 playgroups and child minders.

PPA, as it develops and grows in an area, throws up people who are ready to help outside their own playgroups, and whose experience is most valuable. The adviser should aim to use them, have them as her team, build them up, train them in fact. People need to be needed, they are willing to help, and they have so much to give; they know their own localities and can interpret to the adviser in her early days.

Some of them are potential tutors, and most advisers will be aware of the acute shortage of suitable tutors for play-group courses. How can they widen the available tutoring force? Several methods have been tried.

1. As already outlined, existing tutors spot likely tutors on their own courses, and as these potential tutors attend the course for the second time they watch the interplay between tutor and students, and constantly ask themselves, 'Would I have answered that question that way? How would I have handled this or that situation?'

Discussion with the tutors after each session helps them to gain confidence and widen their understanding. They will already have had playgroup experience, and the reason for inviting help will have been their general attitude and maturity towards both children and adults.

Sometimes someone will have a particular gift, without previous training, and her help can be valuable in her particular sphere. She may be able to inspire others to take animals, plants and minerals to the children, and to present them imaginatively. She may have a real flair for art, and an intuitive understanding of what is natural for pre-school children to be producing, backed up by a collection of children's work. She may be able to excite the students into creating a collection of dressing-up clothes that delight the eye and stand up to the hardest wear and tear. She may be able to enthuse students into trying all sorts of musical experiments in the playgroup, or be able to make up stories on the spur of the moment.

183

Everyone with a natural gift and the ability to communicate it should be encouraged to use it.

2. In one area fifteen experienced playgroup people met about six times a term for two years in order to discover what sort of course would be needed to prepare a group of people for tutoring. Actual and potential fieldworkers and tutors continue to pool their experience and resources—hence the name 'resource group'.

Gradually it was realized that far from being armed against all questions, queries and opinions because they knew all the right answers the essential quality in a tutor was that she should be as open to learning as the students, not trying to convert people to this or that way of thinking, but helping them to observe children and learn from *them;* not trying to raise the standards directly but seeking first to relax rigid attitudes in order that the playgroup should benefit as a direct result of increased awareness and understanding. Gradually the would-be tutors let go of their own needs and came to identify with the needs of their future students.

The second phase was an attempt to identify what the *students* needed, and the simple needs of those new to playgroups seemed to be these: that the tutor had an understanding of the practicalities of a playgroup; that she could steer the group through playing with the activities themselves in such a way that everybody began to identify with children; that she could help them to become sensitive to children, so that they came to *learn* from children rather than wanting to do things to, and for, children; and finally that she could demonstrate how to present each activity, indicate how children might behave and suggest ways of coping with the different situations.

In short, it is practical experience and human understanding that are called for as well as specific knowledge. And many playgroup people are rich in both these qualities; but they need to come together with their local adviser to work out with her the various ways of explaining, demonstrating, and answering questions in such a way that no one is made to feel discomfort, neither are they left thinking in rigid terms of right and wrong.

3. One hard-pressed adviser works in an area where few are qualified, but many are playgroup experienced and wise in their

understanding of mothers and children. She has welded such people into a team, but did not wish to use the word tutor (lest real tutors were rightly shocked, and her team was immediately paralysed by the grandness of the word), so she called them caretakers, and asked them to help her to take care of new people coming together to learn a bit more.

4. Another course for would-be tutors ran once a week for a year under the skilled care of a psychologist, who was also the playgroup-experienced mother of four children.

Each of these experiments has been a genuinely creative effort by people-on-the-spot to consider their local need and their resources. Clearly, we must all proceed with caution, but the level of help needed by a group of mothers wanting to know about mixing paint, laying-out equipment, making dressing-up clothes and other practicalities does not render the risk a very great one. The point on which to be clear is that of the giving of advice: it needs to be understood that this sort of help is responsible, practical and friendly, as one playgroup leader to others; it does not presume to be training.

Playgroup advisers often feel it would be a help if instead of endlessly taking playgroup leaders to relevant groups in their cars, they could telephone the leader of such a group and say, 'Could you pop over to such-and-such a playgroup and help them to work out how and where they could have water play?' We are working towards meeting such a need: branches of PPA are willing to help advisers in any way they can.

FOOTNOTE 1976

The shortage of playgroup-experienced tutors continues. We note that there are many able people supervising splendid playgroups, who relate warmly to children and adults, and who feel ready to move out of the playgroup into the wider field of the playgroup movement. But if anyone suggested that they might like to think about being area organisers or tutors they would draw back saying 'I'm not ready.' Some need wider experience; others need this together with longer personal maturation time.

We are already running a few experimental fieldwork courses in order to meet both these needs, and it is interesting to see how naturally the playgroups experience spirals up and out into the wider sphere of observation, relationships and responsibility.

Chapter 14

The way ahead

The future of the playgroup movement lies in building on the ideal of equality of opportunity for *families* to grow in stature and happiness, as the community focuses its attention on the provision of the best possible playgroups.

PLAYGROUP COURSES

1. Priority must be given to the preparation of more tutors to run playgroup courses. All too few understand the aims of playgroups, and those who do are being worked to the point of exhaustion.

Since it is of paramount importance that the social service aspect of playgroup work shall include the educational aspect relating to the quality of play and the quality of the tutoring it is essential that both the Department of Health and Social Security *and* the Department of Education and Science are jointly involved at central level, together with PPA, in discussing all training projects.

2. Pressure to institute a graded series of nationally recognized courses should be resisted until the country is covered with a network of tutors who really understand playgroups; then it will be possible to consider the form and content of a series of courses specifically planned *to accept people as they are* and to help them to prepare, start, maintain, and improve playgroups suited to their environment and ever growing capabilities.

3. Time may well prove that colleges of further education are not the most appropriate siting for all playgroup courses. Many mothers need to have the course held in the hall where their

186

playgroup will be started; they need to *see* where everything is going to be placed, and how they can adapt and improvise.

If, administratively, it continues to be necessary for courses to be run in further education buildings it will also be necessary for provision to be made for the right tutors to be engaged even if their qualifications seem to be 'wrong'.

It is already clear that a PPA inspired training for tutors will be needed. As one tutor said, 'We need such patient and percipient help if we are to move on from the "I want to make playgroups better/good/educationally right" motivation to the "I want to help the mothers to grow in knowledge and understanding of children." ' *The simple truth is that one cannot achieve the first without first accomplishing the second.* We shall need to weld together the nursery school teachers' knowledge of the under-fives; the social workers' knowledge of families under stress; and PPA's knowledge of the wide variety of normal family life and child rearing patterns in many different areas, and the impact of playgroups in their local communities.

While PPA works towards this nationally, such tutors as are locally acknowledged to be right should be allowed to continue their tutoring. For example, some 'just mothers' are better able to explain mother-involvement than some sociologists.

4. Materials for practical sessions need to be made available at no extra cost to the students, or to the tutors. At the moment many tutors are buying paper, paint, clay and flour out of their own pockets for two very good reasons.

They feel that the playgroup people are already doing more than their fair share of money-raising for the children's sake, and they do not wish to ask them to pay for materials as well as for their courses and their fares (many people travel around sixty miles to attend each session).

At a very human level they know the real pleasure that each mother feels as she makes her way to the course unencumbered by children, shopping baskets or playgroup paraphernalia. This is not sentimental rubbish, it is a simple statement of fact: mothers of young families hardly ever experience the physical freedom of being able to walk at their own pace with their hands uncluttered. If the course provides an attendant playgroup, then still less do the mothers want to arrive with children, handbags, rolls of paper, jars of paint, and seven-pound lumps of clay.

5. No one should be debarred by lack of money from learning how to run a playgroup for the children and the community. Courses should be free or at a nominal cost: at the time of writing only four education committees charge no fees.

6. No course should offer a certificate of anything other than attendance; and even that should be modest enough not to offer the temptation to have it framed and hung on the wall as 'my certificate'.

7. There should be no written examinations in connection with playgroup courses.

8. No tutors should be appointed to playgroup courses without having spent a whole morning in each of at least four playgroups. Wherever possible the PPA area organizer or branch secretary would nominate four playgroups of widely different types, in order that the tutor shall understand the live situations to which her knowledge is being applied.

9. Tutors should visit at least a proportion of the same playgroups both before and after a course. It is perfectly possible to feel that one has taught well, only to see from the static playgroup that one has not, apparently, taught anything at all. Tutors need *to assess themselves, rather than to assess the playgroup leaders*; it is a question of 'nothing that I have done, or said, has improved the playgroup itself (though I am sure the new attitudes have improved the home situation), so how can I re-think, re-plan and originate some new approach in order that there *shall* be a carry-over from the course to the playgroup?'

10. Playgroup courses should be run, whenever possible, in conjunction with a good demonstration playgroup. A crèche, assembled from the children of the students who attend the college each day, is *not* a playgroup. The demonstration playgroup needs a nucleus of regular local children, with their mothers helping in the daily running of the group. The additional numbers can be made up by adding the three- and four-year-old children of the mothers who attend courses.

Children under three are unlikely to settle without their parents; and even if they did, they should not be in the playgroup but in a specially prepared nursery unit.

PREMISES FOR PLAYGROUPS

1. Rents should be subsidized at a uniform level in each locality. At the moment it is possible to find within a few miles of each other some playgroups paying 60p per morning, and others paying £3 per morning; the cost has to be passed on to the children. Sometimes the excessive rent is due to the expense of the heating system, and a grant towards changing the heating system should be considered.

In one case the system was such that the playgroup could not be heated unless the large adjoining church was heated at the same time: the playgroup catered largely for non-English speaking immigrant children, where the need was great and finance very limited.

Should not local authorities, the churches and the community relations councils all come together to discuss who uses these halls and who, singly or jointly, might be responsible for the capital outlay that would enable them to be used economically?

2. All existing buildings housing playgroups should give equal weight to the storage needs of everybody. At the moment too many hall committees are defending the rights of former societies and clubs to maintain what they already have, and it is left to the playgroup to raise the money for outside storage sheds.

If there is no more room within the building for storage space should the firstcomers not feel jointly responsible for the plight of the latecomer? If all the various hall-users joined the playgroup in raising the money for external storage space a community spirit could be engendered which would prevent the playgroup from feeling that it was an interloper.

3. No new church, community buildings, youth clubs, health centres or similar buildings should be planned without consideration being given to the needs of a playgroup. This does not merely relate to the provision of suitable toilet accommodation

and storage space, but to details of planning which would cost little, but yield a high return in ease of working.

For example, consideration might be given to the following ideas.

Storage rooms could be designed so that they opened off the hall and, when emptied of their equipment, could form small book rooms, with books held flat by plastic-covered wires lining the walls. Or such rooms could become home corners.

Long low flaps (about ten feet long by three feet high) could be recessed into the walls in a corner; these could be swung out and bolted into the floor to form a home corner that neither sagged nor collapsed as do clothes-horse screens, nor restricted space as do bought Wendy-houses.

Provision is needed for an area to have flooring of a type that could stand water, sand, clay, and paint, without damage to a dancing surface.

Extra electric points could be put in the kitchen, with two or three ironing boards available, so that lonely mothers could deliver their children to the playgroup and then gather together to do a weekly chore in happy companionship.

Adjoining rooms could lead off the hall, offering scope for the running of a playgroup course, or for the informal gathering of mothers who wish to stay and chat. This latter point is particularly relevant in rural areas where mothers may have travelled up to fifteen miles to bring the children, and they prefer or need to stay until the end of the session. If they all congregate in the playroom the children tend to become adult-accessories instead of experiencing the joy of being in a child-centred environment.

NEW COMMUNITIES BEING PLANNED

1. Planners should think in terms of the differing needs of real families, including one-parent families. And society should ask itself if any under-fives should be part of a large group in full day care.

2. Realistic provision should be made for storage in all buildings intended to serve the community. Under-fives need a vast

amount of equipment and materials; teenagers need sports and hobby equipment, and space for stripping down bikes; jumble has to be stored; kitchens need more cooking facilities (one church team in a new town has built up a real community spirit by enlisting the help of neighbours to cater for most of the weddings and socials).

3. Parents need to be planned for as part of pre-school and school life. A parents' room may isolate more than it involves parents, and the space might be put to better use in creating, bays in classrooms and corridors.

4. Waiting rooms should be planned with children in mind.

5. No families with young children should be forced by circumstances to live in high-rise flats. Where this has already happened the mothers are very occasionally offered the use of an empty flat to be used as a playroom. The authorities concerned sometimes tell me that 'It never works, the whole thing always falls through': and mothers have told me, 'We're afraid to make a go of it, because when we ask to be taken out of the flats they may say "Which lot are you in? The X-block? Well, you're all right aren't you, you've got a playroom. I'm afraid we must give priority to families who have no play provision at all."'

It is no use offering an empty flat unless (a) the inhabitants are assured that they are still priority cases to be moved into houses; and (b) a salary is provided for someone to act as catalyst and playgroup leader, for many of these mothers are in such a state of nerves that the shouldering of this sort of responsiblity could be too much for most of them initially.

6. In private housing estates it should surely be obligatory to provide adequate play provision for all age groups; also for consideration to be given to the needs of children indoors. One housing scheme at the drawing-board stage has included a small storage room with full length window and built-in window seat; while young couples have few possessions to store, the toddler can have this as a playroom, and the mother can sit on the window seat and feel herself to be part of the world passing by the large window as she keeps an eye on the toddler playing.

OUTDOOR PLAYSPACES

It is useless to plan for provision for the under-fives without bearing in mind the needs of their mothers. If mothers are to be encouraged to take their children to a prepared playspace they need:

1. A wind-free shelter, reached by the afternoon sun, with good visibility in all directions. Seats need a back rest, and if they are placed in a curve rather than a straight line it is easier for mothers to chat as they keep an eye on their children. A windbreak for prams is also necessary.

2. Paths wide enough to take the wheels of a pram for twins; a surface so hard that the heels of afternoon-shoes will not sink into black stickiness during a heat wave; a surface sufficiently smooth and curved not to hold water.

3. An accessible lavatory, wash basin and drinking water. When planning the lavatories it should be borne in mind that these will be used not only by children but by heavily expectant mothers who need more room than is often allowed.

4. No sweet kiosks near enough for every afternoon walk to become a battle of wits and wills as the mother tries to hold out against buying sweets and is intimidated by the fear that her offspring might make a scene in front of the other mothers (who are similarly trying to hold out).

5. An enclosure round the play area that allows them the peaceful certainty that no child can get out.

Children need:

1. Grassy mounds and hollows—growing legs need the challenge of a small hill to climb; growing intellects need the surprise of the different viewpoint from the top; growing independence needs the illusion of being alone as the downhill stagger temporarily blots mother from view.

2. A hard-surfaced area for push-and-pull toys and tricycles. If there was a wide path round the perimeter of the play area the rising fives could cycle further and faster than they would

be able to do among the gently pottering toddlers on the main hard area.

3. Sand pits, preferably two side by side with a paved area between them: after the digging and sandcastle stage the next progression of play is often the carting of sand from one place to another. If the sand pits are adjoining then the sand can be transferred from one definite place to another. If the sand pit is near trees, or if cats and dogs roam the area at night, it helps to have a wire-netting-covered wooden frame to drop over the pit at night.

4. Earth for digging if possible. It may look untidy, but digging in the sand pit is not a true substitute for digging like the men on their allotments.

5. Shallow water, in full view of the accompanying adults, for paddling and sailing small boats.

6. Flowers for picking. Nothing grand calling for money or labour, just a fingerhole poked between the rails or posts of the fencing round the enclosure with nasturtium and everlasting pea seeds dropped in and trodden down. Even if only a few of them survived the various hazards there should still be a plentiful supply of flowers for several months. There are children in towns who have never in their lives picked a flower. This is a serious deprivation and a real effort should be made to provide such an experience.

7. Small walls and steps for balancing and jumping.

8. Climbing apparatus, a small slide and swings. All these need a surface below them that will minimize the danger of falls, and prevent the formation of a quagmire in wet weather. A deep gravel soak-away pit covered with a good layer of sand might be the answer.

SUPERVISED PLAYSPACE FOR THE UNDER-FIVES

The GLC Arts and Recreation Committee (formerly the GLC Parks Department) have blazed a trail worthy of being widely copied. The original play parks were so successful that the Play Leadership Organizer, Mr H. S. Turner, extended the scheme so that the huts and playgroup leaders could be available for the under-fives before the older children flocked in after school.

Originally it was envisaged that the mothers and their children could enjoy the play facilities under the sympathetic supervision of the playgroup leader from 3 p.m. until the school children arrived. However, the scheme was so popular that the opening time was put back two hours and One O'Clock Clubs were born. Later, the premises were offered to playgroups in the morning before the One O'Clock Clubs took over for the afternoon session. It is important to understand the difference between these two sessions, for each has its own unique value worthy to be preserved.

ONE O'CLOCK CLUBS

Admission to these is free, and there is no limitation on numbers any more than there is on the beach at the seaside, but the parents are required to stay with their children. The reason for this is twofold.

1. All ages under five are welcome, and there is no register or set time to come and go: this free and easy movement would make it impossible for even the most experienced playgroup leader and her assistants to be responsible for the children.

2. It was quickly realized that if the mothers had to stay they came happily prepared to do so and began to relax, make friends, and thoroughly enjoy themselves.

The playgroup leaders set out all the materials, toys and equipment (for which no charge is made) and offer the unobtrusive help that enables each child to have the illusion of real freedom. The mothers, with or without younger members of the family, gather informally in groups to chat, knit or do nothing peacefully. In the summer they spread themselves over the grass, in winter they find seats in the play huts. At weekends fathers come with, or instead of, mothers and the universal cry is 'It's lovely to have somewhere where you are all welcome; usually nobody wants to know you if you have toddlers.'

There are twenty-nine of these One O'Clock Clubs, and the

newest ones have opened in purpose-built premises; there is a large covered area for prams, and a small room for the accompanying adults leading off the playroom, but in full view of the children by virtue of its large communicating window. The afternoon I spent there three of the young mothers breezed in with the identical comment, 'I live for this moment each day!'

Many of the families live in high flats and they all said the same thing, 'After dinner you can get everything tidy to go back to, then you can come here until four-ish and when you get back the children are ready for tea and bed so nothing gets messed up before your husband comes in after work.' Another comment that I heard repeatedly was, 'There's no point in coming out if you haven't got somewhere definite to go to. It's no fun just pushing a pram round a park, specially in the winter, and walking round the houses or shops is worse still.'

PLAYGROUPS IN ONE O'CLOCK CLUB PREMISES

The premises must be inspected and the playgroup registered with the Social Services Department as for any other playgroup: this means that numbers will be limited, a register will be kept, and the children who come will do so regularly. The premises are generously offered rent free, and the play equipment and materials are also provided without cost, which reduces the cost to the parents well below that of playgroups which have to cover rent, heat and equipment.

Since parks must remain open to the public, children will use the outside playspace during the time that the playgroup is in session, but they will not join the playgroup children inside.

The children in the playgroup will be primarily in the three to five years age group and although mothers will be required to settle in their children they are not obliged to stay once the child is happy to be left alone. The rota system of helpers usually applies.

Some families want and need the informal gathering together of adults and all children under five that the One O'Clock Clubs offer; some want and need the more formally constituted framework and aims of the playgroup; some want and need both and are sensible enough to realize that if Johnny has attended playgroup on Wednesday and Thursday mornings then the family visits to the One O'Clock Clubs will be more appropriate on the other afternoons of the week.

What matters is that more buildings and surroundings should be provided that can serve this dual purpose for those hours of the day when they would otherwise be empty.

URBAN AID FOR EDUCATIONAL PRIORITY AREAS

A bird's eye view of one such scheme will illustrate the human distress that could be avoided.

There were already three nursery schools and twenty classes attached to infant schools in one urban area, also the Save the Children Fund were running a number of playgroups before the first parent-inspired playgroups struggled into existence. And it was a very real struggle, not only financially but in terms of human courage and perseverance. Vicars, health visitors, PPA advisers and course tutors gave every possible encouragement and support, and slowly the playgroups stabilized, and even began to prosper cautiously. Courage and confidence grew and a PPA branch was formed so that the playgroups would have the support of each other, and something to offer to new playgroups.

Then came Urban Aid: thousands of pounds, and a local authority adviser to spend the money in setting up twenty new playgroups. It does not take much imagination to identify with the feelings of those who, until then, had been happily coping with their do-it-yourself playgroups. The very human cry of 'It isn't fair!' went up as they saw that the new groups were given their equipment; given rent-free halls; given the services of a playgroup leader, who was herself given the local playgroup course tuition, for which the other playgroup leaders had paid.

The adviser was immediately aware of this blank dismay, hurt and anger, and begged that the original parent-inspired playgroups should also be beneficiaries under the Urban Aid scheme. The only concession that she was able to get was permission to inject money into any of the earlier playgroups if it became apparent that they would collapse without help. Six months later two of these playgroups applied for help urgently, stating that they would collapse unless it was forthcoming.

196

There are various possible explanations for these crises.

1. The groups may have been shaky before the advent of Urban Aid. Since they were firmly established in the beginning this could have been due to the fact that the strong supportive help of the local vicar or social worker or tutor or other mature personality fell away. No such group can ever be considered to be established once and for all, and encouragement must continue indefinitely.

2. The groups may have been disheartened by the withdrawal of children from their vital waiting list with the explanation, 'I think we'll wait and get into one of the cheaper playgroups.' These mothers had pronounced themselves willing and able to pay 12p or 15p a session at the time of registration, but why pay this if you can get it for 5p?

Once disheartened, the newly acquired enthusiasm, pride and independence can dwindle so low that the energy to kindle the spark in others is lost. Only those who have done it know just how many sandwiches, cakes and cups of coffee have to be made to raise enough money to buy a £50 climbing frame. It takes the gilt off the gingerbread to see new playgroups equipped by the simple process of lifting things out of a van.

3. Real anger may have engendered bloody-mindedness. The argument may have been 'Right! It doesn't pay to help yourself. If we hadn't done something to get things going they would have done it for us—so let them get on with it! Let's fold up, and start again the easy way!'

Careful thought is needed before Urban Aid money is spent locally on playgroups lest it divides rather than strengthens existing community life.

Is the aim to help as many children as possible? Or is it to reach these same children *and their parents*, with a view to the long-term benefit to both generations and the community in which they live? If it is the latter, then several stages must precede the opening of playgroups and no pressure should be put upon anyone to set up a given number within a time limit.

It must never be assumed that all the mothers in these areas are drop-outs, and the fact that it is often difficult to involve them initially should not tempt people into taking the short cut of starting playgroups 'for the children' in the hope that mothers might come along afterwards. It is extremely unlikely that there is not a small nucleus of parents willing to be involved from the beginning, but it may well take a social development officer or playgroup adviser some time to find them and foster their awareness that a playgroup would be a good idea.

The work of a social development officer should be complemented by that of an adviser. The former can winkle out the enthusiasts; call large or small meetings; sit through each one, ready when advice or guidance are needed; pave the way towards the next stage and generally be available as a signpost or a temporary leaning post. There comes a moment when the original idea becomes a firm goal and then the adviser will be needed. What sort of things do children want in a playgroup? What do they cost? Where do they come from? Can anything be made, or scrounged, or improvised? The need for a playgroup course arises spontaneously, and the adviser will need to meet it herself, know where to send the mothers or, better still, know who to bring in to the group so that the course can be run in the hall where the playgroup will open.

The first playgroup in the area is the one that takes the time, patience and skill to establish. Once it is flourishing these are the parents who will become the local experts willing and eager to be visited by those about to start, and continuing to work in close contact with the social development officer and the adviser, who will quietly see to it that this enthusiasm and the various growing abilities are channelled and used to the full.

In several areas, branches of PPA have been given grants under Urban Aid, phases II and III, to further the work that they have already started in their voluntary capacity.[1] The strength of PPA locally is that the members do not think in terms of underprivileged children living in deprived areas, but rather of families living in homes that make life exhaustingly difficult for all of them. Genuine warmth and friendship can sometimes bring about the same result as that achieved by the professional.

The adviser, social development officer and playgroup people will need to give as much time and thought to the courses, and

[1] Now, in 1976, we are up to Urban Aid phase XV, and have been given greatly increased grants from phase XIII onwards.

the preparation of people to swell the tutoring team, as they do to the playgroups themselves. Some of the extra members of the team are likely to be found among the local playgroup people themselves.

Halls may need to be improved, rents subsidized, playgroup leaders' salaries subsidized, an ever-growing team of tutors and demonstrators paid, travelling expenses provided for those who help to nurse along new playgroups, large items of equipment may need to be provided (or money raised on a fifty-fifty basis), courses need to be free. Money is indeed needed. But in each case where money is given, careful, extensive and sensitive local research should precede allocation so that the greatest benefit can be derived from the money that is available.

RESEARCH NEED

1. If parents were helped to help their own children, thereby growing in happiness and insight themselves, would this enable the parent-child relationship to be a living and growing (instead of a strained and dwindling) source of support to both generations? If so, would this last up to the critical adolescent years?

2. What is best for children: to take them away from their homes and minister to them expertly? Or to take parents and children together and help the parents to reach certain set standards in their learning and playgroup provision? Or to take parents and children together and help them to undertake a venture that stretches them all, but stops short of straining them, even if the standard falls short of professional?

3. Can we help adolescent boys and girls to have some awareness of childhood and play? Experience of including them in playgroups indicates that many still need to play themselves. Could playing, watching children play, and discussing what they see and feel help to prepare them towards a parenthood that will not blindly reproduce their own childhood? Many youngsters come into playgroups, but there is little hope of their gaining much from it unless they are prepared for their visits, and can discuss them afterwards.

In 1962 one of the PPA pioneers started a playgroup in a southern port, and when this was firmly established she started another, with the help of the first group. This led to a third

199

group, and still the personal link between them all was maintained. By 1970 there were eighteen playgroups, catering for 1000 children. The eight uptown playgroups help to subsidize the ten downtown playgroups, and the finances are balanced thus. In the comparatively well-off areas the cost to the children is 15p per session, which makes it possible for the charge in the other areas to be kept down to 5p or 7½p. Thirty children pay nothing, and twenty children are paid for by Urban Aid money. Approximately a third of the mothers are involved in the playgroups in one way or another.

The top pay for playgroup leaders is £1 per session, and 50p for the regular helpers. In some playgroups two people prefer to share the leadership by working together each session; they then receive 75p each. The 1970–1 balance sheet showed that income had been £6360 and expenditure £6336. Constant fund-raising is necessary, for the shared fun and a sense of purpose as much as for the money to add to equipment. Jumble sales are the most popular means of raising money, but other methods are constantly being tried and tested.

The pre-Christmas party meeting is a highlight in each playgroup year. The original pioneer attends each one with a bottle of sherry tucked under her arm, and everyone feels that this occasion for planning the children's party is a party for the adults concerned.

The project has met needs other than the obvious ones.

1. Saturday morning groups have been started, with the help of the Social Services Group. These sessions are attended by children between two and thirteen years, and the skilled and mature adults present have noted that family grouping occurs to the benefit of all. It is also noted how eagerly the older children play with the playgroup activities.

2. Food education is badly needed, and gratefully accepted when it is offered in friendly chat. Some mothers spend a large amount on food, yet their children come within the clinical definition of undernourished, or are showing signs of a specific deficiency.

3. Some mothers brought to the verge of battering their babies are able to express their fears and overcome the urge in the supportive help that is offered.

4. Some families have been kept together when the mother is confined to bed with a breakdown. Playgroup mothers collect the children, return them, help with meals and generally hold the fort.

5. Mothers unable to rise early in the morning (for a variety of reasons) gratefully allow the children to be called for, dressed, given breakfast and taken to the playgroup. The mother, rested, then fetches her children at the end of the session.

The woman who is personally responsible for all this still leaves home at 8.30 a.m. each day, visits playgroups (on foot or by bus) until 3.30 p.m., and then returns home to cope with the finances. New playgroups are visited every day, most are visited once or twice a week, but no playgroup is ever visited less than once a fortnight. The mothers know that if they want to speak to her they have only to attend each playgroup session until she arrives, and she will listen and advise (if asked) for as long as they need her. Only during the eighth year did she draw any money for herself, and then only enough to cover bus fares.

Could money be made available for the following purposes?

1. To monitor the whole project, following up not only the children but also the parents.

Once roused from loneliness and apathy by being drawn into the life of the playgroup, do these parents maintain their contacts in the community and their desire to go on learning? Are they able to find new outlets for their energies and abilities?

2. To stabilize the project.

At the moment it is heavily dependent on the health and strength of this one voluntary worker. If this woman were officially appointed to her self-imposed job she would be able to build up a team of part-time paid helpers who could help her to maintain and further the work.

It seems wasteful not to safeguard this pocket of exemplary self-help; still more wasteful not to use it for research purposes.

PRE-SCHOOL PLAYGROUPS ASSOCIATION

I firmly believe that the country cannot afford either to take over, or to allow the collapse of this valuable voluntary movement. Help is needed, and the following points could be considered:

1. Many of the voluntary members on the national executive committee are working very nearly full time; so are other members in the field. This cannot go on for two reasons. Firstly, the expenses for phone, post and public transport are only a fraction of the true cost. Help is needed in the house if the housewife is occupied elsewhere; washing needs to be sent to the laundry, or someone has to be paid to do the ironing; 5p a mile for the family car is unrealistic. Secondly, husbands are growing angry on their wives' behalf. They are proud of their wives, and glad to see them developing their talents; this is not the area of their anger. It is the growing awareness that their wives are being 'used'. At first they were sympathetic that officials would not take the volunteers seriously; then they were proud that confidence and co-operation were developing; now they are angry where this willing help is being used so freely without expenses being met realistically.

It seems unlikely that PPA will ever be able to afford to pay realistic expenses, let alone a token payment such as playgroup leaders receive. The area of work and service spreads; these women's consciences will not allow them to say 'No sub, no help!' for they know only too well that it is the ones who will not or cannot pay a subscription who are likely to be the ones most in need of experienced help. If this work is to go on, key voluntary workers must at least be assured of a generous expense allowance.

It is hoped that local members and the local authorities could work out something between them.

2. A substantial grant should be made to PPA for the specific purpose of stabilizing playgroups started in pockets of real deprivation. Recourse to local Urban Aid money is of limited use here, for this approach is delayed by planning permission, waiting and implementation. The machinery is too slow and cumbersome to help in those instances where the right person happens to be in the right place at the right time and, catching the moment, helps the local parents to launch their playgroup. The initiator will stay by it, but needs money to ensure that the

fees are not too high, nor the fund-raising demands too heavy to be met without turning the venture into a marathon of endurance. The playgroup leader will need to be subsidized in these areas but the mothers should still contribute something towards her salary.

CHURCHES

The Church of Scotland has appointed two deaconesses as full-time advisers on playgroups, who both advise and help new playgroups and also advise ministers and churchmen and women in the playgroup movement. To help the deaconesses in their work a playgroup committee has been set up, composed of ministers, guildswomen, playgroup leaders and representatives of other relevant committees.

South of the border the only appointment of a playgroup adviser at Diocesan level, as far as I know, is at Derby.

The Church of England Board of Education set up a Children's Council's research officer.

The Methodist Women's Fellowship and Youth Department set up a working party, at which PPA was represented, to produce a paper, 'The Churches' Role in Pre-school Activities', which would be a guide to those in the church who are concerned with the pre-school child and playgroups.

The Religious Society of Friends (Quakers) have a Child Poverty Action Group with a particular interest in community action through playgroups: their Race Relations Committee and Friends Educational Council also both sponsor playgroups.

More recently an Inter-Church Playgroup Working Party has been set up, and meetings so far have been attended by representatives of the Church of England Board of Education, the Methodist Youth Department and Women's Fellowship and Young Wives, the London Congregational Union, the Presbyterian Church of England, the Friends' Educational Committee, the Baptist Union, the National Board of Catholic Women, and PPA.

Innumerable tales could be told of the generosity and dedication of many clergy and local church communities, but one real source of concern remains.

Is child development included in theological training? This

203

query is prompted by a number of personal encounters with 'religion' in playgroups, culminating in one tragic example which ultimately led to this basic query: a sincere vicar stipulated that the playgroup could take place in the church hall if he could come in and tell the three great Christian stories at the appropriate seasons. The Christmas story was a great success: children understand about babies being born, and this very special Baby made a deep impression. Months later, a mother told me, she collected her distressed four-year-old from the playgroup, and on reaching the safety of home the distress broke into hysteria. When the child was able to speak she said 'Mummy, you know the Baby that was born at Christmas? Well, they've killed him with a hammer and nails.' Clearly the vicar did not understand that because his Baby was identified with 'my baby at home', so his cross and nails were identified with the playgroup carpentry bench. The child was left with fear and horror because her stage of development made it impossible to have any concept of spiritual triumph and glory.

Help seems to be needed on two fronts.

1. A priest or minister needs to understand, in simple practical terms, just how much a child can or cannot understand at each stage of development. The child is father to the man, and the foundations of learning have far-reaching consequences.

2. Playgroup courses should give more time to explaining how we can keep a child's response to beauty, his awe and wonder, his reverence for life whether it be another child, a pet, an insect or a flower, alive and growing.

3. Talks on discipline need to underline the necessity for community rules, and the knowledge of when to break them very occasionally for the stronger claim of love; the necessity to convey to a child that we love him, even when we decline to allow him to act in such a way that he hurts somebody else. We need to help mothers to understand that it is not kind to shield a child from grief and suffering, for it is by accepting them and living through them with loving support that we come to grow towards the fullness of ourselves.

'Religion' has no place in a playgroup; but 'the harvest of the Spirit: love, joy, peace, patience, kindness, goodness, fidelity, gentleness and self-control' is the essence of such a venture, whatever the creeds of those who play and work together.

EDUCATION AND SOCIAL SERVICES DEPARTMENTS

Scotland has set an example worthy to be followed. The Social Work Services Group continues to sponsor two-day conferences for all the voluntary area organizers of Scottish PPA. Under skilled leadership the area organizers are working out their thoughts on their present role.

There was a time when members all over the country pressed for a playgroup leaders' training that gave a nationally recognized diploma. But the situation is changing, and it is coming to be recognized that the turnover of playgroup leaders has certain advantages.

1. No one becomes so deeply entrenched that the parents begin to feel that it is 'her' playgroup rather than 'our' playgroup.

2. There is a constant lookout for local talent and it is precisely this that encourages people to grow into roles that they once thought were beyond them.

3. Certainly playgroup courses are necessary, whether or not people were previously trained; but this is not at all the same thing as a nationally recognized diploma. The idea that 'they won't work without the stimulus of a certificate to aim at' is simply not true; they are avid seekers after knowledge and are joyously aware of the growth of their understanding. More thought is needed on this subject, but possibilities begin to appear.

If playgroup leaders are to be encouraged to rise up from the local community, then the local playgroup courses must be very good indeed, and the support offered to all the individual playgroups must be equally sound. No one adviser can do all this individual visiting, and if the tutors and area organizers undertake this they will need some form of recognized course.

No existing training has the vital dimension of learning to work simultaneously with parents and children in a playgroup setting, *with the responsibility of drawing out the latent abilities in both generations, to the detriment of neither.*

It is now time for local social services and education authorities to accord community playgroups, together with their attendant playgroup courses, a permanent place in their future planning for the under-fives and their families. Playgroups, and their supportive voluntary workers, need the recognition and help of *both* authorities.

The climate of society is such that a strong bias towards education in playgroups might lead to a type of over-compensation linguistically and intellectually that could be detrimental to the total personality growth of the children; it could also lead parents into the uncomprehending copying of systematic training patterns that would damage the all-important parent-child relationship, fail to achieve their goal of 'getting the children on', and deepen their sense of failure as parents and as people. Similarly, a strong bias towards social services could result in playgroups being the happy centre of community activity, but with the rather superficial happiness that does not ask too many questions about the real value to the children of all that stems from the playgroup.

What is needed is a very careful balance between the two. Certainly there must be happiness, *but the quality of everything that stems from the playgroup is largely dependent upon the quality of play of the children within it*. Many of us who have spent years tutoring playgroup courses or working in playgroups are certain that it is not too late for parents to learn about children and childhood—happily and fruitfully because, in some cases for the first time in their lives, a passionate desire to learn is aroused. It is not too late for them to change the negative attitudes and behaviour that result from the unthinking copying of their own childhood models. But if this is to happen they must first glimpse a satisfying alternative which can act as a catalyst for this process of regeneration, hence the importance of selecting the right playgroup leaders, area organizers, tutors and advisers.

We must be careful not to give parents the impression that those who missed out during the first five years of their life have 'had it'. The love of one's children, and a new vision, are motives strong enough to start parents on a new cycle of personal growth, in which both they and their children can grow nearer to the fullness of themselves as unique human beings.

FOOTNOTE

At the end of June 1972, PPA held a Local Authority Conference at Westminster which was opened by the Secretary of State for Social Services, Sir Keith Joseph, with a major policy statement on provision for the under-fives. At the same time he announced his Department's substantial grant to PPA. The grant included £9500 for capital works, including the second phase of adaptation at Alford House, the new H.Q., an embryonic playgroup centre that members had been cleaning, decorating and furnishing from donations since the plunge was taken to rent it and move in last May. There was also up to £45,000 in a year for revenue costs. This grant will now allow us, initially, to appoint four full-time Training Officers and four full-time Development Officers.

The Department's letter confirming the grant states: 'The Government are making this grant because they recognize the importance of playgroups in the development and care of children and the mother and child relationships. We wish to see playgroups expanding, particularly in the priority areas of social deprivation, and improving in quality. It is hoped that this grant will speed the process.'

We believe that it will, and it is in affirmation of our belief that parents have a far greater potential than they realize that we asked for money to promote development and our various courses side by side.

It is an essential part of the ethos of PPA that playgroups and playgroup courses are inseparable—together, they form the basis of our concept of children and parents learning and growing together.

FOOTNOTE 1976

The DES grant is now £20,000.

The DHSS grant is now £161,000 plus a £13,480 capital grant for equipping Regional Offices.

The Welsh Office grant is now £18,000.

It is not possible to record details in a footnote, but we should like to say how grateful we are—not only for the money, but for the continual personal support that is given to so many of us so generously.

Book List

This is not a list of 'good' books, let alone 'the best books'; it is not even a list of the books that I happen to approve of, or like; it is nothing more than a list of books that people of different types and temperaments, living in different communities, have mentioned with significant frequency as having been 'marvellous'. This can be taken to mean that some of these books may ring a bell for some of you, and if the first two that you try add nothing to your understanding or personal relief it doesn't necessarily follow that the others will not be your type either.

UNDERSTANDING CHILDREN

Understanding the Underfives, Baker, Donald, Evans
Feeling and Perception in Young Children, Chaloner, Len, Tavistock.
The Magic Years, Fraiberg, Selma, Scribner.
The Special Child, Furneaux, Barbara, Penguin.
The Child's World, Hostler, Phyllis, Pelican.
Babies and Young Children, Illingworth, R. S. and C. M., Churchill.
The Behaviour of Young Children, Isaacs, S., Kegan Paul.
The Nursery Years, Isaacs, S., Kegan Paul.
Childhood and After, Isaacs, S., Kegan Paul.
Social Development in Young Children, Isaacs, S., Kegan Paul.
Pre-school and Infant Art, Jameson, K., Studio Vista.
The Continuum, Liedhoff, Jean, Duckworth.
Understanding Children, Morris, Beverley, A. H. Reed.
The Psychology of Childhood and Adolescence, Sandström, C. I., Pelican.
Your Three-year Old (*Four-year Old* etc), Tavistock Clinic, Corgi Minibook.
The Country Child, Uttley, A., Puffin.
The New Childhood, Wright, Erna, Allen Wingate.

UNDERSTANDING THE FAMILY

Four Years Old in an Urban Community, Newson, J. and E., Penguin.
Patterns of Infant Care in an Urban Community, Newson, J. and E., Penguin.
Pre-school Years, van der Eyken, W., Penguin.
The Child, the Family and the Outside World, Winnicott, D. W., Penguin.
Family and Kinship in East London, Young and Wilmott, Pelican.

The novels for children (ten to twelve years) by William Mayne give a picture of one sort of family life that could add to the experience of those with different childhood memories.

UNDERSTANDING CHILDREN IN THE FAMILY, AND THE FAMILY IN THE COMMUNITY

Childhood and Adolescence, Hadfield, J. A., Penguin.

UNDERSTANDING HANDICAPPED CHILDREN, AND THEIR PARENTS

Born Illegitimate, Crellin, Pringle, West, National Foundation for Educational Research.
Stigma, the Experience of Disability, Ed. Paul Hart, Geoffrey Chapman.
Oliver Untwisted, Payne, Margaret, Arnold, last printing 1944.
Living with Handicap, Younghusband, Birchall, Pringle, Johnson Reproductions.
Dibs: In Search of Self, Axline, Virginia; Pelican.

SHARING THE BOAT IN WHICH SOME OF US FIND OURSELVES

The Feminine Mystique, Friedan, Betty, Dell.
Between Parent and Child, Ginott, H. G., Staples Press.
How to Survive Parenthood, le Shan, Eda, Random.
Talks with Mothers, Growth and Guidance, Spock, B., Bodley Head.
The Longest Weekend, Arnold, Honor, Hamish Hamilton.
In the Springtime of the Year, Hill, Susan, Hamish Hamilton.

REMEMBERING BACK TO CHILDHOOD

Over the Bridge, Church, Richard, Heinemann.
The King of the Barbareens, Hitchman, Janet, Peacock.
George, Williams, Emlyn, Hamish Hamilton.
Cider with Rosie, Lee, Laurie, Penguin.
Robin, Storr, Catherine, Young Puffin.
George, Turnbull, Agnes S., Young Puffin.
Child of Our Times, Wall, W. D., National Children's Homes.
Daddy Long Legs, Webster, Jean, Hawthorn.
Miss Clare Remembers, 'Miss Read', Penguin.

FOR THOSE WHO WISH TO KEEP ALIVE IN THEMSELVES, AND THEIR CHILDREN, A SENSE OF WONDER

The Creative Imagination, Barnes, Kenneth C., Friends Home Service.
The Sense of Wonder, Carson, Rachel, Harper and Rowe, N.Y. and Evanston.
The Prophet, Gibran, Kahlil, Heinemann.
Your Growing Child and Religion, Lee, R. S., Pelican original.
Children in Search of Meaning, Madge, Violet, S.C.M.

FOR THOSE INTERESTED IN PLAY AT HOME, OR IN THE PLAYGROUP

Teaching Young Children, Beyer, Evelyn, Pegasus.
Mother's Help, Ed. Susan Dickinson, Collins.

THE PLAYGROUP MOVEMENT

Play with a Purpose for the Under Sevens, Matterson, E. M., Penguin.
Playing, Learning and Living, Roberts, Vera, Black.
Playgroup Activities, PPA Publications, Alford House, Aveline Street, London, SE11 5DJ.

FOR THOSE INTERESTED IN STARTING A PLAYGROUP

PPA publications, from Alford House, Aveline Street, London, SE11 5DJ.

FOR THOSE INTERESTED IN LANGUAGE

Language and Exploration (series of four, Young Children Learning), Yardley, A., Evans.
Language, Speech and Communication, PPA Publications.

FOR THOSE WHO WONDER HOW AND WHEN TO HELP CHILDREN TO UNDERSTAND SEX

Sex in the Childhood Years, Edited by Isadore Rubin and Lester A. Kirkendall, Fontana.
What to Tell Your Child About Sex, Proposed by Child Study Association of America, Allen and Unwin.

FILM LIST

Children and Clay	PPA teaching film		Black/white, silent, 16 mm and 8 mm
Children and Dough	,, ,, ,,		,, ,, ,,
Children and Water	,, ,, ,,		,, ,, ,,
Children and Dry Sand	,, ,, ,,		,, ,, ,,
Children and Wet Sand	,, ,, ,,		,, ,, ,,
Children and Paint	,, ,, ,,		Colour, silent, 16 mm and 8 mm
Children and Apparatus	,, ,, ,,		Black/white
Children and Home Play	,, ,, ,,		Black/white
Children and Waste Materials	,, ,, ,,		Colour
Children and Hammering	,, ,, ,,		Colour

All the above films run for approximately ten minutes, and are specifically intended to be shown twice, with discussion between the two showings. A booklet has been compiled of the typical comments made after the first showing, and of the quite different comments made after discussion and the second showing, of each of the six films. We urge those wanting to show the films to read this before doing so; it is obtainable from PPA.

210

Films can be hired from Concord Film Council, Nacton, nr. Ipswich, Suffolk, or bought from PPA, Alford House, Aveline Street, London, SE11 5DJ

Hire charge
16 mm £1·10 (£1·50 for *Children and Paint*, the only one in colour)
 8 mm £1 (£1·40)

Purchase price
16 mm £30 (£40 for *Children and Paint*)
 8 mm £20 (£30)

Films of Playgroups

Looking at Playgroups. Colour, 25 minutes. From Contemporary Films Ltd, 55 Greek Street, London, W.1. or The Scottish Film Council.

Before School. Colour, 15 minutes. From Devon County Education Committee, County Hall, Exeter.

A Place to Play. Colour, 20 minutes, 8 mm. From Concord Film Council, Nacton, Ipswich.

Films of Playgroup Practice

Improving Your Playgroup, in five parts:

Lay-out	Black/white, 20 minutes
Sand and Water	From: BBC
Books and Imaginative Play	T.V. Enterprises,
Painting	Villiers House,
Questions and Answers	Broadway, London, W.5.

Parents in Playgroups
Two playgroups are seen through the eyes of a family in Bootle and a family in Honiton. They explain how the playgroups have met their different needs.

Country Children
This film shows a two- and a four-year-old enjoying a wonderful family life helping their parents on the windswept hills of their farm. The only real deprivation is that of the companionship of children of their own age, and a playgroup two mornings a week is invaluable. But when they meet other children Stuart and Roger are shocked into silence and immobility at first and react as warily as startled animals to this strange new environment.

This is not a film about 'rural deprivation', or even 'rural playgroups'. It is quite simply a film about country children who have a great deal to teach us.

Both films are 16 mm, colour, and run for 30 minutes. They can be hired from The Churches Television and Radio Centre, Hillside, Merry Hill Road, Bushey, Watford WD2 1DR at £6·60 plus VAT, postage and insurance.

211

THE PLAYGROUP MOVEMENT

Your kids join you join
A playgroup of our own
Both films are 16 mm, black/white, run for 30 minutes and can be hired
from Concord at £3·20 and £4·40 respectively, plus p.p. and VAT.

EQUIPMENT AND TOY FIRMS

Arnold, E. J. and Son, 12 Butterley Street, Leeds 10.
Educational Supply Association Ltd, Pinnacles, Harlow, Essex.
Galt, James and Co. Ltd, Brookfield Road, Cheadle, Cheshire.
Goodwood, Havant, Chichester, Hants.
Hope, Thomas and Sankey Hudson Ltd, Pollard Street, Manchester 4.
Margros (Berol Ltd), Monument Way West, Woking, Surrey.
Philip and Tacy Ltd, 69 Fulham High Street, London S.W.6.
Pirongs, P. J. and S. Ltd, Leigh Road, Chichester, Sussex.
Playgroup Supplies Ltd, Stoke Canon, Exeter.
Whittle, R. W. Ltd, P. V. Works, Monton, Eccles, Manchester.